Essential Legal System and Legal Services for SQE1

Ian Bowden and Zaman F. Kala

Routledge
Taylor & Francis Group
LONDON AND NEW YORK

Designed cover image: © Getty Images

First published 2024
by Routledge
4 Park Square, Milton Park, Abingdon, Oxon OX14 4RN

and by Routledge
605 Third Avenue, New York, NY 10158

Routledge is an imprint of the Taylor & Francis Group, an informa business

British Library Cataloguing-in-Publication Data
A catalogue record for this book is available from the British Library

Library of Congress Cataloging-in-Publication Data
Names: Bowden, Ian, author. | Kala, Zaman F., author.
Title: Essential legal system and legal services for SQE1 / Ian Bowden and Zaman F. Kala.
Description: Abingdon, Oxon [UK] ; New York, NY : Routledge, 2024. | Series: Essential law for SQE1 | Includes index.
Identifiers: LCCN 2023059031 | ISBN 9781032564388 (hardback) | ISBN 9781032564371 (paperback) | ISBN 9781003435525 (ebook)
Subjects: LCSH: Law—England—Examinations, questions, etc. | Law—Wales—Examinations, questions, etc. | Legal Services—England—Examinations, questions, etc. | Legal Services—Wales—Examinations, questions, etc. | Law—England—Sources. | Law—Wales—Sources. | Courts—England. | Courts—Wales. | Solicitors Qualifying Examination. | LCGFT: Study guides.
Classification: LCC KD663 .B69 2024 | DDC 349.42076—dc23/eng/20240129
LC record available at https://lccn.loc.gov/2023059031

ISBN: 978-1-032-56438-8 (hbk)
ISBN: 978-1-032-56437-1 (pbk)
ISBN: 978-1-003-43552-5 (ebk)

DOI: 10.4324/9781003435525

Typeset in The Sans
by Apex CoVantage, LLC

Access the SQE1 Series Companion Website: www.routledge.com/cw/sqe

Essential Legal System and Legal Services for SQE1

Essential Legal System and Legal Services for SQE1 explains the key principles of the English and Welsh Legal System, sources of law and legal services in a clear, concise and easy-to-follow style. Principles are introduced and illustrated with reference to practical examples. The book explains the importance of, and the workings of, the Legal System of England and Wales, including the hierarchy of the courts, sources of law and the regulation of legal services.

The book provides a clear and structured approach with opportunities to apply the relevant principles to the law. It also includes a range of interactive features, including:

- Revision points: Each chapter concludes with a concise list of key revision points.
- Multiple choice questions: Each section of the book provides multiple choice questions following the SQE1 question format (with answers to enable you to test your knowledge). Further multiple choice questions and answers are also provided on the companion website.

Part of a series of books aimed at those who are preparing for SQE1, this concise and accessible text provides a clear understanding of the key principles of the Legal System and Legal Services of England and Wales, and enables you to test your assessment skills.

Ian Bowden is a practising solicitor advocate with many years of experience working in legal practice. He is also a senior lecturer at the University of Chester and has experience of delivering on a wide range of undergraduate and postgraduate modules. He has successfully developed the LLM with SQE programme at the University of Bolton.

Zaman F. Kala is a lecturer and accredited mediator in the School of Law and Policing at the University of Central Lancashire, where he teaches on the undergraduate and postgraduate programmes. Prior to embarking upon a career in academia, Zaman worked as a fee earner at a leading firm of solicitors, specialising in insurance litigation and dispute resolution.

Essential Law for SQE1

Series editor: Wendy Laws

Essential Law for SQE1 is a series of concise textbooks aligned to the latest SQE1 curriculum. Providing candidates with an accessible summary of the core principles in each area of law, the style of each book is precise, with bullet-point lists summarizing key information and revision points concluding each chapter. The books also features multiple choice questions with answers, example problem questions and a glossary of key cases.

Essential Tort Law for SQE1
Wendy Laws

Essential Dispute Resolution for SQE1
Ben Waters

Essential Business Law and Practice for SQE1
Bill Davies

Essential Land Law for SQE1
Mohammad Sabuj

Essential Legal System and Legal Services for SQE1
Ian Bowden and Zaman F. Kala

For more information about this series, please visit: https://routledgetextbooks.com/textbooks/sqe

To Beverley, Rachel and our families for your support and for putting up with the sound of typing.

Contents

Table of Cases xiii
Table of Statutes xvii

Introduction 1

Part 1: The Legal System of England and Wales 3

1 **The Legal System of England and Wales** 5
1.1 SQE1 Syllabus 5
1.2 Chapter Overview 5
1.3 The Characteristics and Features of a Legal System 5
1.4 The Rule of Law – Basis and Application 7
1.5 The Origins of Law Within the English Legal System 7
1.5.1 The Norman Conquest 8
1.5.2 The Magna Carta 8
1.5.3 The Growth of Parliament 9
1.5.4 The Rise of Judicial Balance 9
1.5.5 The Bill of Rights 10
1.5.6 The Representation of the Peoples Act 1832, 1867 and 1884 11
1.5.7 European Law from the European Communities Act 1972 through to Assimilated Law 12
1.6 The Civil and Criminal Legal Systems of England and Wales 13
1.6.1 What is Criminal Law? 13
1.6.2 What is Civil Law? 14
1.6.3 Administrative Law 14
1.7 The Constitutional Position of the UK 15
Chapter 1 Revision Points 16
Multiple Choice Questions 17

Part 2: Sources of Law – Primary Legislation and Statutory Interpretation 19

2 Primary Legislation 21
2.1 SQE1 Syllabus 21
2.2 Chapter Overview 21
2.3 An Introduction to Parliamentary Sovereignty 21
2.3.1 The Enrolled Bill Rule 22
2.3.2 The Implied Repeal Rule 22
2.3.3 Constitutional Statutes 24
2.4 What Is Primary Legislation? 24
2.4.1 Creation of Acts of Parliament 26
2.4.2 The Structure of a Statute 28
2.5 Interpreting an Act of Parliament 31
2.6 Statutory Instruments and Byelaws 31
2.6.1 Statutory Instruments 32
2.6.2 Byelaws 32
2.7 Senedd Cymru 33
2.7.1 The Legislative Process (Senedd Cymru) 33
Chapter 2 Revision Points 35
Multiple Choice Questions 36

Part 3: Statutory Interpretation 39

3 Statutory Interpretation 41
3.1 SQE1 Syllabus 41
3.2 Chapter Overview 41
3.3 Divining Parliamentary Intention – The Statutory Interpretation Framework 41
3.4 Statutory Interpretation Rules 42
3.4.1 The Literal Rule 44
3.4.2 The Golden Rule 45
3.4.3 The Mischief Rule 46
3.4.4 The Purposive Approach 47
3.4.5 The Interaction of the Rules 48
3.5 Rules of Language and Construction 48
3.5.1 Noscitur a Sociis 49
3.5.2 Ejusdem Generis 49
3.5.3 Expressio Unius est Exclusio Alterius 50
3.5.4 Application of the Language Rules 50
3.6 Legal Presumptions 50
3.7 Aids to Interpretation 51
3.7.1 Internal Aids 52
3.7.2 External Aids 52
3.7.3 *Pepper v Hart* [1993] AC 593 53
Chapter 3 Revision Points 54
Multiple Choice Questions 55

Part 4: The Courts and Their Role in the Doctrine of Judicial Precedent 57

4 Judicial Structures Within the Courts 59
4.1 SQE1 Syllabus 59
4.2 Chapter Overview 59
4.3 An Overview of Judiciary and the Court System 59
4.3.1 Overview of the Court System of England and Wales 60
4.3.2 Supreme Court 61
4.3.3 Senior Courts of England and Wales 61
4.3.4 Lower Courts 61
4.3.5 Tribunals 61
4.4 The Civil Courts 62
4.4.1 County Court Personnel 62
4.4.2 High Court Personnel 64
4.5 The Criminal Courts 64
4.5.1 Magistrates' Court Personnel 64
4.5.2 Crown Court Personnel 65
4.5.3 Juries in the Crown Court 65
4.6 Further Court Personnel 66
4.6.1 Senior Judiciary 66
4.6.2 Tribunal Personnel, Arbitrators and Mediators 67
Chapter 4 Revision Points 68
Multiple Choice Questions 69

5 Sources of Law – The Courts and Precedent 71
5.1 SQE1 Syllabus 71
5.2 Chapter Overview 71
5.3 Introduction to the Common Law 71
5.3.1 Criticisms? 72
5.3.2 Parliamentary Sovereignty and the Common Law 72
5.3.3 Example 72
5.4 The Doctrine of Judicial Precedent 73
5.5 Precedent in Practice 73
5.5.1 Ratio Decidendi and Stare Decisis 73
5.5.2 Precedent Case Example 74
5.5.3 Precedent Advantages and Disadvantages 76
5.5.4 Precedent and Hierarchy 76
5.5.5 Judicial Precedent and Statutory Interpretation 78
5.5.6 Precedent, Courts and Tribunals 79
Chapter 5 Revision Points 82
Multiple Choice Questions 83

Part 5: Hierarchy, Appeals and Jurisdiction 85

6 **Civil Courts** 87
6.1 SQE1 Syllabus 87
6.2 Chapter Overview 87
6.3 The Role of the County Court 87
6.4 Appeals From the County Court 88
6.5 The High Court 89
6.5.1 King's Bench Division 90
6.5.2 Chancery Division 90
6.5.3 Family Division 91
6.5.4 Appeals From the High Court 91
6.6 Rights of Audience 93
6.7 Tribunals 94
6.7.1 Local Authority Tribunals 95
6.7.2 Governmental Tribunals 95
6.7.3 HM Courts and Tribunals Service Administrated Tribunals 95
6.8 The Senior Courts 96
6.8.1 The Court of Appeal 96
6.9 The Supreme Court 97
6.10 Judicial Committee of the Privy Council (JCPC) 97
Chapter 6 Revision Points 98
Multiple Choice Questions 99

7 **Criminal Courts** 101
7.1 SQE1 Syllabus 101
7.2 Chapter Overview 101
7.3 The Hierarchy Within the Criminal Courts 101
7.4 The Criminal Justice Process 102
7.4.1 The Police 102
7.5 The Process of Investigation 103
7.5.1 The Crown Prosecution Service 105
7.5.2 The Criminal Procedure Rules 106
7.5.3 The Magistrates' Court 106
7.5.4 The Crown Court 108
7.6 The Criminal Appeals Process 109
7.6.1 Appeals From Magistrates' Court 110
7.6.2 Appeals From the Crown Court 111
7.6.3 Appeals to the Supreme Court 112
7.6.4 Appeals to the Judicial Committee of the Privy Council 113
Chapter 7 Revision Points 113
Multiple Choice Questions 114

Part 6: Legal Services 117

8 Regulating Legal Services 119
8.1 SQE1 Syllabus 119
8.2 Chapter Overview 119
8.3 Defining Legal Services 120
8.4 The Solicitors Regulation Authority (SRA) 120
8.5 Authorisation 122
8.5.1 Reserved Legal Activities 122
8.5.2 Firm-Based Authorisation 123
8.5.3 Individual Authorisation 124
8.6 Professional Indemnity Insurance 124
8.7 Unregulated Providers 125
Chapter 8 Revision Points 125
Multiple Choice Questions 126

9 Overriding Legal Obligations 127
9.1 SQE1 Syllabus 127
9.2 Chapter Overview 127
9.3 Equality Act 2010 127
9.3.1 Protected Characteristics 128
9.3.2 Prohibited Conduct 132
9.3.3 Solicitors' Obligations as Service Providers 136
9.4 The Money Laundering, Terrorist Financing and Transfer of Funds (Information on the Payer) Regulations 2017 (SI 2017/692) 139
9.4.1 Purpose and Scope 139
9.4.2 Due Diligence Requirements 142
9.4.3 Reporting Requirements 144
9.5 The Proceeds of Crime Act 2002 145
9.5.1 Offences 145
Chapter 9 Revision Points 147
Multiple Choice Questions 148

10 Financial Services 151
10.1 SQE1 Syllabus 151
10.2 Chapter Overview 151
10.3 Financial Services Regulatory Structure 152
10.3.1 The Financial Conduct Authority 152
10.3.2 The Prudential Regulation Authority 152
10.4 The Financial Services and Markets Act 2000 and the Legal Profession 153
10.4.1 The General Prohibition 153
10.4.2 The Financial Promotion Prohibition 154
10.5 Regulated Activities 154
10.5.1 The Four Tests 154
10.5.2 Are You in Business? 154

10.5.3 Specified Investments 155
10.5.4 Is There a Specified Activity? 155
10.5.5 Exclusions 156
10.6 Professional Body Exemption 158
10.7 SRA Financial Services (Conduct of Business Rules) 159
Chapter 10 Revision Points 161
Multiple Choice Questions 162

11 Funding Legal Services 165
11.1 SQE1 Syllabus 165
11.2 Chapter Overview 165
11.3 Introduction 165
11.4 Funding Options 165
11.4.1 Privately Funded Matters 165
11.4.2 Fixed Fees 166
11.4.3 Conditional Fee Agreements (CFA) 167
11.4.4 Damages-Based Agreements (DBA) 168
11.4.5 Legal Expenses Insurance 169
11.4.6 Third Party Funding 170
11.4.7 Legal Aid Funding 171
Chapter 11 Revision Points 173
Multiple Choice Questions 174

12 Answers to Multiple Choice Questions 177
12.1 Chapter Overview 177
12.2 Chapter 1 – The Legal System of England and Wales 178
12.3 Chapter 2 – Primary Legislation 179
12.4 Chapter 3 – Statutory Interpretation 180
12.5 Chapter 4 – Judicial Structures Within the Courts 181
12.6 Chapter 5 – Sources of Law – The Courts and Precedent 182
12.7 Chapter 6 – Civil Courts 183
12.8 Chapter 7 – Criminal Courts 184
12.9 Chapter 8 – Regulating Legal Services 185
12.10 Chapter 9 – Overriding Legal Obligations 186
12.11 Chapter 10 – Financial Services 187
12.12 Chapter 11 – Funding Legal Services 188

Index 189

Table of Cases

Addy & Sons v Dumbreck [1929] AC 358–5.5.3, n36 **79n3**
Adler v George [1964] 1 All ER 62–3.4.2 **45**
Adobe Systems Inc v Netcom Distributors [2012] EWHC 1087 (Ch) – 3.4.5 **48n5**
Andrea Francovich and Others v Italian Republic, Joined Cases C-6/90 and C-9/90, [1991] ECR I-5357–1.5.7, n4 **12n5**
Anisminic Ltd v Foreign Compensation Commission [1969] 2 AC 147–3.6, n26 **51n12**
Arkin v Borchard Lines Ltd [2005] EWCA Civ 655–11.2.6 **171**
Arthern v Ryan Air DAC [2023] EWHA 46 (KB) – 5.6 **000**
Austin v Mayor and Burgesses of the London Borough of Southwark [2010] UKSC 28–5.5.1, n35 **78n2**
Beswick v Beswick [1968] AC 58 – n30 **53n16**
BH (AP) (Appellant) and another v The Lord Advocate and another (Respondents) (Scotland) [2012] UKSC 24–2.3 **24**
Bourne (Inspector of Taxes) v Norwich Crematorium Ltd [1967] 1 WLR (QB) 696–3.5.1 **49**
British Railways Board v Herrington [1972] AC 877–5.5.3, n36 **79n3**
Bushell's Case (1670) – 1.5.4 **10**
Caldwell v Maguire & Fitzgerald [2001] EWCA Civ 1054–5.5 **74**
Casamitjana Costa v League Against Cruel Sports [2020] ET/3331129/2018–9.3.1.6 **130**
Citation of Authorities (2012) [2012] 2 All ER 255–5.6, n42 **000**
Colchester Estates v Carlton Industries [1986] Ch 80–5.5.3, n39 **80n6**
Commission for Racial Equality v Dutton [1989] IRLR 8–9.3.1.5 **130**
Conisbee v Crossley Farms Ltd and others [2019] ET/3335357/2018–9.3.1.6 **130**
Donoghue v Stevenson [1932] AC 562–5.5, 5.5.1 **78**
Ealing LBC v Race Relations Board [1972] AC 342–9.3.1.5 **130**
Edinburgh and Dalkeith Railway co v Wauchope (1842) 8 CL & Fin 710 – n8 **22n2**
Eweida v United Kingdom [2013] ECHR 37, [2013] IRLR 231–9.3.1.6 **130**
Fisher v Bell [1961] 1 QB 394–3.4.1 **44**
Foster v Diphwys Casson Slate Co (1887) 18 QBD 428–3.5.1 **49**
Fothergill v Monarch Airlines Ltd [1981] AC 251–3.7.2, n29 **53**
Fuller's Case (1607–08) – 1.5.4 **9**
Ghaidan v Godin Mendoza [2004] UKHL 30–3.8, n32 **000**
Grainer Plc and Others v Nicholson [2009] UKEAT/0219/09ZT – 9.3.1.6 **130**

Heydon's Case (1584) 3 Co Rep 7–3.4.3 **46**
Jackson and others (Appellants) v Her Majesty's Attorney General (Respondent) [2005] UKHL 56–2.3, n9, n12 **22n3, 27n6**
Mandla v Dowell Lee [1983] 2 AC 548–9.3.1.5 **130**
Matthews v Ministry of Defence [2003] UKHL 4–5.6 **000**
Maunsell v Olins [1975] AC 373–3.4.5 **48n6**
National Assistance Board v Wilkinson [1952] 2 QB 648–3.6, n25 **51**
R v Jogee [2016] UKSC 8 (joint enterprise) – 7.6.3 **112**
Partridge v Crittenden (1968) 2 All ER 421–3.4.1, **44**
Pepper v Hart [1993] AC 593 – n14, 3.4, 3.7.3, **43, 53**
Pickin v British Railways Board [1974] AC 765 – n8 **22n2, 3**
Practice Statement [1966] 1 WLR 1234–5.5.1 **78–79, 83**
R (HS2 Action Alliance) v Secretary of State for Transport [2014] UKSC 3–2.3 **24**
R (Miller) v Secretary of State for Exiting the European Union [2017] UKSC 5–1.6, n6 **15n6**
R (on the application of Miller and another) v Secretary of State for Exiting the European Union [2017] UKSC 5–2.3 **24**
R (on the application of Worcestershire County Council) (Appellant) v Secretary of State for Health and Social Care (Respondent) [2023] UKSC 31–5.6 **000**
R (on the application of Worcestershire County Council) (Appellant) v Secretary of State for Health and Social Care (Respondent) [EWCA] Civ 1957–5.6 **000**
R v Clarence (1888) 22 QBD 23–5.5 **76**
R v Clarle [1949] 2 All ER 448–5.5 **76**
R v Golds [2016] UKSC 61 (diminished responsibility) 7.6.3 **112**
R v Letby [2023] – 7.5.4, n43 **109n1**
R v Miller [1954] 2 QB 282–5.5 **76**
R v O'Brien (Edward) [1974] 3 All ER 663–5.5 **76**
R v R [1991] UKHL 12, [1991] 3 WLR 767–5.5 **74–75**
R v Reid [1973] QB 299–5.5 **76**
R v Secretary of State for Health ex parte Quintavalle (on behalf of Pro-Life Alliance) 2003 UKHL 13–3.4.4 **47**
R v Steele (1976) 65 CR App R. 22–5.5 **76**
R v Uddin [2017] EWCA Crim 1072–3.5.2 **49**
R(O (A Child) v Secretary of State for Home Department [2022] UKSC 3 – n16, 3.7.2, n28 **43n2, 52n14**
Re Allister et al [2023] UKSC 5–2.3 **24**
Richardson v DPP [2019] 4 WLR 46–3.5.2 **50**
Robinson v Secretary of State for Northern Ireland [2002] UKHL 32–3.7.3 **54**
Rootes v Shelton [1968] ALR 33–5.5 **74**
Serco v Lawson [2006] ICR 250 (HL) – 3.6, n23 **50**
Smith v Hughes [1960] 1 WLR 830–3.4.3 **46**
The Boucraa [1994] 1 AC 486 (HL) 525–3.6, n24 **51**
The Case of Proclamations (1610) 12 Co Rep 74; 77 ER 1352 – n3 **10n3**
Thoburn v Sunderland City Council [2002] EWHC 195 (Admin); [2003] QB 151 – n7, 2.3 **21n1, 24**

Vauxhall Estates v Liverpool Corporation [1932] 1 KB 733 (DC) – n10 **23n4**
Whiteley v Chappel (1868) LR 4 QB 147–3.4.1 **45**
Wilson v Secretary of State for Trade and Industry [2003] UKHL 40–3.7.3, n31 **54**
Young v Bristol Aeroplane Ltd [1944] KB 718, [1944] All ER 293–5.5.3, n38 **80n5**

Table of Statutes

Abortion Act 1967–2.4 **25**
Access to Medical Treatments (Innovation) Act 2016–2.4 **25**
Act of Settlement 1701–1.5.4 **10, 15**
Advanced Research and Invention Agency Act 2022–2.4 **25**
Anti-social Behaviour, Crime and Policing Act 2014–2.4 **25**
Arbitration Act 1996–4.6.2 **67**
Bill of Rights 1689–1.5.5, 1.7, 2.3 **5, 15, 21–22**
Children and Families Act 2014–6.5.3 **91**
Civil Partnership Act 2004–9.3.1.4 **129**
Commonwealth Development Corporation Bill 2016–17–2.4 **26**
Constitutional Reform Act 2005–1.5.4, 1.7, 4.3.4.6.1, 6.8 **7, 10, 15, 59, 61, 66–67, 79, 96**
Consumer Rights Act 2015–2.4 **26**
Contracts (Rights of Third Parties) Act 1999–2.4, 3.4 **26, 43**
Coronavirus Act 2020–2.4 **25**
County Courts Act 1867–6.3 **87**
Courts and Legal Services Act 1990–11.2.3, 11.2.4 **167, 169**
Crime and Courts Act 2013–6.5.3 **91**
Criminal Appeals Act 1968–7.6.2 **111**
Disability Discrimination Act 1995–9.3, 9.3.1.2 **127**
Domestic Violence, Crime and Victims Act 2004–3.5.2 **49**
Equal Pay Act 1970–9.3 **127**
Equality Act 2010–3.3, 9.1, 9.2, 9.3, 9.3.1, 9.3.1.1–9.3.1.9, 9.3.2, 9.3.2. 1–9.3.2.5, 9.3.3, 9.3.3.1–9.3.3.3 **42, 127–128, 131, 134–136,139**
European Communities Act 1972–1.5.7, 2.3 **12–13, 22, 24**
European Parliament Elections Act 1999–2.4.1 **27**
European Union (Withdrawal) Act 2018–1.5.7, 5.5.3 **13, 81n8**
Financial Services and Markets Act 2000–10.1, 10.4, 10.4.2, 10.5, 10.5.1–10.5.2, 10.6, 10.6.1, 10.7 **151–156, 162–163, 187**
Financial Services and Markets Act 2000 (Regulated Activities) Order 2001–10.6.4, 10.6.5 **155–156**
Government of Ireland Act 1914–2.4.1 **27**
High Speed Rail (West Midlands-Crewe) Act 2021–2.4 **25**
Highgate Cemetery Act 2022–2.4 **25**
House of Lords Act 1999–2.4.1 **27**
Human Fertilisation and Embryology Act 1990–3.4.4 **47**
Human Rights Act 1998–1.7, 2.3, 3.8 **15, 22, 24, 83**
Judicature Acts 1873–1875–4.3, 5.5.1, 5.7, 6.8 **61**
Legal Aid, Sentencing and Punishment or Offenders Act 2012–11.1, 11.2.7, 11.2.7.1, 11.2.7.2 **165**
Legal Services Act 2007–6.6, 8.4, 8.5.1, 8.7 **93, 120, 122, 125, 185**

Life Peerages Act 1958–2.4.1 **27**
Local Government Act 1972–2.6 **33**
London Olympic Games and Paralympic Games Act 2006–2.4 **26**
Magistrates' Courts Act 1980–1.6 **13, 111**
Magistrates' Courts Act 1980–7.5.1 **13, 111**
Marriage Act 1949–9.3.1.4 **129**
Mental Health Act 1983–6.7 **95**
Merchant Shipping Act 1988–1.5.7 **12n4**
Misrepresentation Act 1967–5.3 **72**
Monken Hadley Common Act 2022–2.4 **25**
Occupiers' Liability Act 1984–5.5.2 **79**
Offence Against the Persons Act 1861–1.6 **13**
Official Secrets Act 1920–3.4.2 **45**
Parliament Act 1911 and 1949–1.7, 2.4, 2.4.1 **15**
Police and Criminal Evidence Act 1984–7.5 **104–105**
Prices of Goods Act 1939–3.4.1 **44**
Proceeds of Crime Act 2002–9.1, 9.5.9.5.1, 9.5.1.1–9.5.1.3, 9.5.1.3.1–9.5.1.3.6 **127, 145–146, 150**
Protection of Birds Act 1954–3.4.1 **44**
Race Relations Act 1976–1.7, 9.3 **15, 127**
Representation of Peoples Act 2000–1.7 **15**
Representation of the Peoples Act 1832–1.5.6 **11**
Representation of the Peoples Act 1867–1.5.6 **11**
Representation of the Peoples Act 1884–1.5.6 **11**
Restriction of Offensive Weapons Act 1959–3.4.1 **44**
Retained EU Law (Revocation and Reform) Act 2023–1.5.7 **13**
Sentencing Act 2020–2.4 **26**
Services (Price Control) Act 1941–3.4.1 **44**
Sex Discrimination Act 1975–1.7, 9.3 **15, 127**
Sexual Offences (Amendment) Act 1976–5.5 **75**
Sexual Offences (Amendment) Act 2000–2.4.1 **27**
Sexual Offences Act 2003–1.6 **13**
Statutory Instruments Act 1946–2.6 **32**
Succession to the Crown Act 2013–1.7 **15**
Supreme Court Act 1981–6.8 **96**
The Act of Union (Ireland) 1800 (Acts of Union 1800)–2.3 **24**
The Act of Union 1707–2.3 **24**
The Appellate Jurisdiction Act 1876–4.3 **61, 76, 82**
The Companies Act 2006–2.4 **26**
The European Union (Notification of Withdrawal) Act 2017–1.6 **15**
The Government of Wales Act 1998–2.7 **33**
The Government of Wales Act 2006–2.7 **33**
The Hunting Act 2004–2.4.1, 2.4.2 **27–28**
The Interpretation Act 1978–, 3.7.2 **53**
The Money Laundering, Terrorist Financing and Transfer of Funds (Information on the Payer) Regulations 2017 (SI 2017/692)–9.4, 9.4.1 **127, 139–140**
The Rent Act 1977–3.8 **000**
The Road Traffic Act 1988–1.6, 2.4 **13, 56**
The Street Offences Act 1959–3.4.3 **46**
The Union with Ireland Act 1800–2.3 **24**
The Wales Act 2017–2.7 **33**
Tribunals, Courts and Enforcements Act 2007–4.3, 4.6.2, 6.7 **59**
Unfair Contract Terms Act 1977–2.4 **26, 72**
War Crimes Act 1991–2.4.1 **27**
Welsh Church Act 1914–2.4.1 **27**

Introduction

This book provides a clear, concise explanation of the Legal System and Legal Services of England and Wales for SQE1. Its focus is on those areas which fall within the assessment specification for the **Solicitors Qualifying Examination Part 1 Functioning Legal Knowledge** ('SQE1').

The style of the book reflects the SQE1 assessment specification:

- The SQE1 assessment requires knowledge and understanding of fundamental legal principles and the ability to apply them.
- Candidates are not required to recall specific case names or statutory provisions (except where they are normally used in practice to describe a legal principle).
- Candidates will be tested on the current law and will not be tested on the historical development of the law.

In order to reflect these requirements, the book explains the current key principles of the law in a clear, easy to follow style. Principles are introduced and illustrated by reference to realistic factual examples. References to key cases and statutes are provided, but without extensive discussion of case law.

Key Features to Assist Learning

Revision points: Each chapter concludes with a concise list of key revision points.

Multiple choice questions: The SQE1 assessment uses multiple choice questions to test understanding of key principles. Multiple choice questions, following the SQE format, are provided at the end of each section of the book (with answers at the end of the book).

A further set of review multiple choice questions and answers is provided at www.routledge.com/cw/sqe

DOI: 10.4324/9781003435525-1

PART

1

The Legal System of England and Wales

1 The Legal System of England and Wales

1.1 SQE1 Syllabus

Historical development of the English Legal System is not examinable under the SQE1 Syllabus as candidates will be tested on the law as it stands. However, you will be required to demonstrate knowledge of the rule of law, assimilated law and an understanding of civil law, criminal law, administrative law and the constitutional position of the UK.

1.2 Chapter Overview

This chapter will provide an overview of the characteristics and features of the English Legal System, and its historical significance. It will begin with the rule of law and its basis, followed by an overview of the origins of the English Legal System. We will consider the Norman Conquest and the Magna Carta, followed by the growth of Parliament, judicial balance and the Bill of Rights 1689.

The chapter will then delve into the development of the Representation of People, European Union Law and the constitutional position in the United Kingdom. There will also be some coverage of the civil and criminal legal systems of England and Wales.

The SQE1 exam will not test your knowledge of the historical development (1.5.1 to 1.5.5) of the law and legal system – but we have included it because understanding that development often makes the current position easier to understand.

1.3 The Characteristics and Features of a Legal System

The characteristics and features of a legal system can vary depending on the specific jurisdiction. However, some common characteristics and features include:
These are just some of the characteristics and features that are commonly found in legal systems. It is important to note that each legal system may have its own

DOI: 10.4324/9781003435525-3

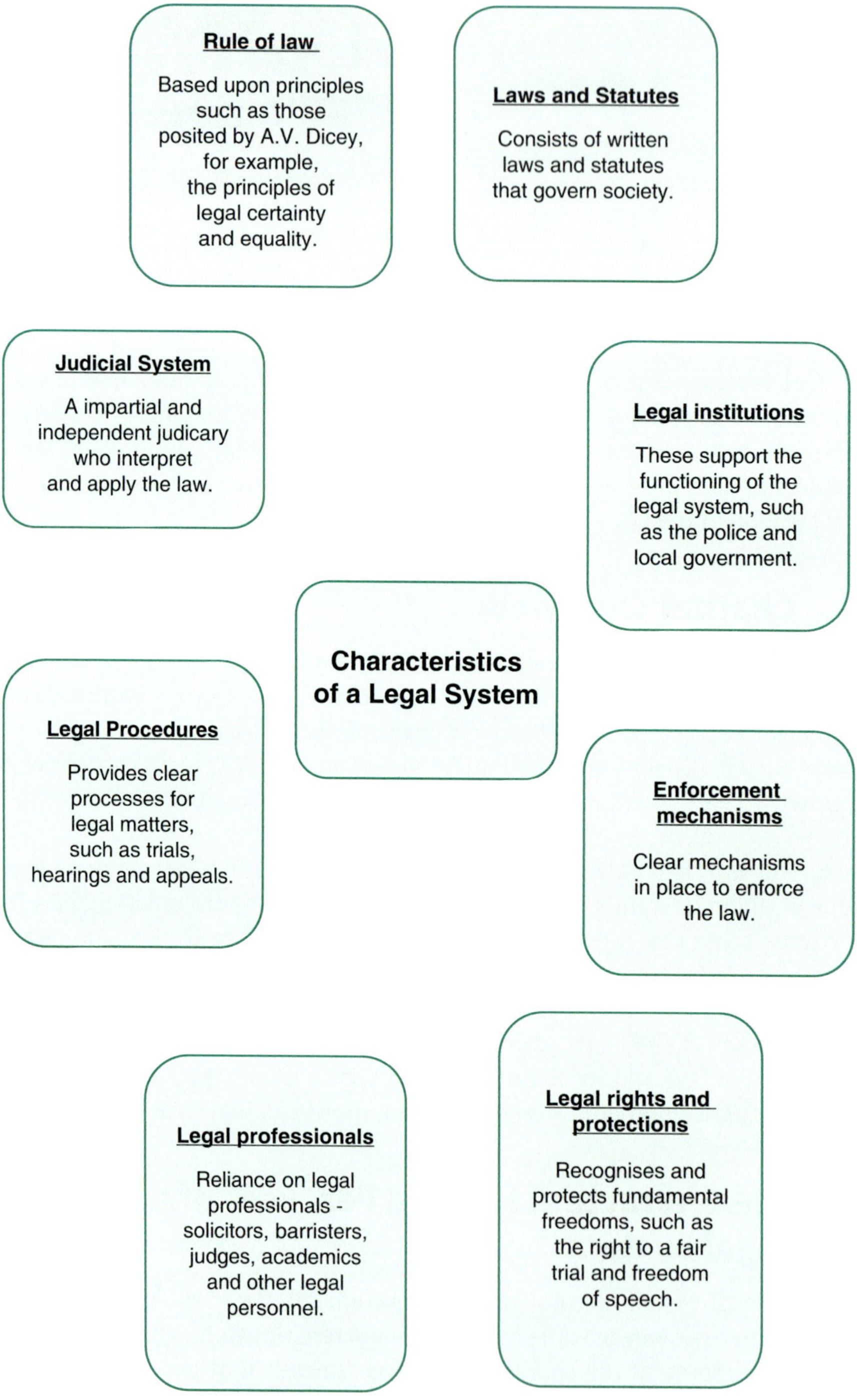

Figure 1.1 A table showing key charactersitics of legal systems

unique aspects and variations based on the specific laws and traditions of the jurisdiction. For example, in the United Kingdom, a Parliamentary system is prevalent, allowing for supremacy.

1.4 The Rule of Law – Basis and Application

As you will already be aware, the rule of law forms a critical element of not just the English legal system but also the many legal systems across the world and is a key factor in most states that have constitutional democracies. The rule of law is widely attributed to A.V. Dicey but has been developed over the years, most notably by Lord Bingham in his lecture on the subject and his eight principles.

The rule of law widely focuses on three broad elements:

1. The principle of legality and legal certainty.
2. Legal equality before the law.
3. Judicial independence.

With respect to legality and legal certainty, this means, simply put, that a state must only act within its legal powers. As such, laws should only be created via those methods that are legal and not arbitrarily. Secondly, laws must be certain to allow those members of a state to note exactly what their legal obligations are.

With respect to legal equality, as Dicey stated, 'no man is above the law.' This provides for the equal treatment of all people before the law, and this is closely linked to fundamental freedoms. It also means that all people, no matter their position in society, will be subjected to the law equally.

Finally, the notion of judicial independence is also critical. This not only ensures that all members of a state have access to justice via a clear legal process but also ensures that their disputes are heard by an independent and impartial judiciary. Fortunately, in the English legal system, judicial independence is guaranteed with a plethora of protections in place due to the clear fusion between the Government and Parliament. The Constitutional Reform Act 2005 has safeguarded judicial independence effectively.

1.5 The Origins of Law Within the English Legal System

The origins of the English Legal System can be traced back to instances of historical and legal significance. Foundationally, the English Legal System is based on over 900 years of legal practice. Under the rule of King Henry in 1200, a centralised system of 'common law' was established. This 'common law' is very much based upon what we use now. The value and robustness of the English Legal System can be traced back to its consistent use over the centuries.

Again, it is important to note that this element will not be tested in the SQE1 exam but provides a context of how the Legal System as we know it has developed.

1.5.1 The Norman Conquest

Historically, whilst the Norman Conquest was significant from a legal standpoint, changes were minimal. The laws introduced by Edward the Confessor were deemed to be sophisticated and encouraged local community law and collective responsibility. There were some changes that were based upon the French system that were introduced after 1070. A significant element of the Norman Conquest was the Domesday survey, which was commissioned by King William on landowners, how such land was held and used, and whether there were any changes from the last day of the reign of King Edward, to as it was in 1086. Such a survey was undertaken by commissioners who held inquests in local courts. The purposes of the survey (very much like the current Land Registry) was to note possession and transfer, value of land and to levy taxes.

1.5.2 The Magna Carta

The Magna Carta was a document that was drafted and issued at Runnymede in the year 1215. The issue of the document was as a result of political turbulence and an uprising of English Barons (nobility). The document itself was a charter, granting rights and freedoms to individuals throughout the kingdom, and such rights were inclusive of the King himself. The importance of this document as a foundation upon which the English Legal System has been built cannot be understated.

Legally speaking, by its very essence, the document provided clarity on how the laws of the land applied to the King and his subjects. Whilst such a rule was customary even prior to 1215, the Magna Carta provided this in writing.

The clauses contained within the Magna Carta have provided a platform for legal principles to be developed within the years thereafter. For example, Clauses 39[1] and 40[2] can easily be related back to current legal practice in terms of rule of law theory itself, due legal process and even habeas corpus. The presumption of innocence and the right to a trial by jury can also be traced back to clauses 39 and 40 of the Magna Carta. Most importantly, it was clear that the document itself sought to express the concept of law being a power in its own right, and that the King and

1 Clause 39 – No free man to be *arrested* and *imprisoned* except by *lawful judgment* of his peers or by the law of the land (Emphasis added).
2 Clause 40 – *Justice* will not be *delayed*, *denied*, or sold (Emphasis added).

his government would also be subjected to such law, by placing limitations on royal authority and preventing the abuse of power by the monarch.

1.5.3 The Growth of Parliament

The very first recording of the term 'parliament' can be traced back to a legal matter whereby King Henry III adjourned a case to a 'parliament.' Interestingly, whilst that did not result in the creation of Parliament as we know it, the term was familiar in medieval England due to its meaning of 'assembly.' The concept of an English King (or Queen) discussing affairs with their subjects was quite normal and referred to as 'councils.' Nonetheless, utilising the term 'parliament,' which originates from the French term '*parelement*' or Latin term '*parliamentum*,' signified that changes were on the horizon. As mentioned in 1.5.2, King Henry endorsed the Magna Carta, and due to his requirement to ask his subjects for taxation regularly, this enabled the concept of parliament to develop, and led to further pressure for the King to invite more of his subjects to the gatherings. In the first instance, assent (similar to that of Royal Assent), was given by the English Barons, in taxation matters. However, as time progressed, King Henry was required to liaise with the lower clergy and representative (members) of towns and counties, who would come to be known as the 'commons.' Clearly, we can see where this is heading!

The fourteenth and fifteenth centuries provided a period whereby Parliament would consolidate its position in the political arena. Legislation was now enacted by 'authority of Parliament' instead of the King, and further confirmed the role that Parliament would go on to play in later centuries with regards to Parliament as we know it.

1.5.4 The Rise of Judicial Balance

The rise of judicial balance can be looked at from two perspectives. The traditional argument regarding the *scales of justice*, and then the independence of the judiciary that flows naturally to ensure impartiality and independence in decision making, which is crucial in the administering of justice and leading to the fair resolution of matters. The concept of access to justice is something that is of vast importance in any legal matter, but its impact today can be traced back.

While England and Wales already had an adversarial system of court process, the King often retained powers in making decisions. In *Fuller's Case* (1607–08), Sir Edward Coke asserted that the common law was supreme and that the King was not able to 'adjudge' any case. Further, if he was to adjudge, then any decisions could not be in conflict with common law precedent and was not capable of arbitrary change by an individual – even if that individual was a King. He stated that his majesty 'was not learned in the laws of his realm of England.' Needless to say, one can imagine how offended the King would be at such a statement!

He further went on to develop such exclusions of the King's and Executive's influence in legal matters in cases such as the Proclamations Cases (1610),[3] where he decided that the King could not utilise his prerogative powers to make or unmake previous laws, citing that the same should be left to Parliament, confirming that English law did not include the King's proclamations, but only those that can be seen as part of the common law and statutory law.

Juries could also be fined by the judges in the event they failed to reach a decision (*Bushell's Case*, 1670). It would also not be until 1836, following the enactment of Prisoners' Counsel Act, where defence lawyers would be able to summarise an address to a jury. In Old Bailey trials, for example, dealing strictly with criminal matters, defence lawyers often would contribute with hearsay evidence and pre-trial confessions, which also allowed defendants to not speak.

The development of trial process and procedure and participation of lawyers at trials allowed for judges to be able to exercise authority, but also one that was aimed at arbitrating the adversarial contest between the parties.

The Act of Settlement 1701 ringfenced the protection of judges by providing statutory protection to their tenures, provided office was held during good behaviour. Further, judges (High Court and Lord Justice of Appeal) were subjected to a formal mechanism in order to initiate their withdrawal – an address to the monarch was required, after agreement by both Houses of Parliament. The notion of independence requires a judge to decide matters independent of all external pressures, to ensure that confidence from the public remains in their decision making, which is to be conducted fairly and in accordance with the rule of law.

Today, following reforms in the Constitutional Reform Act 2005, judges are appointed via a Judicial Appointments Commission (JAC) and also have security of salary, immunity from suit and immunity from criticism.

We will look at the role of judges and the hierarchy of the courts throughout this book.

1.5.5 The Bill of Rights

It is important to note that the 1689 Bill of Rights is not what we know to be a 'bill of rights' akin to those discussed politically regarding the UK's withdrawal from the ECHR charter.

Historically speaking, and furthering our discussion on origins of law, the 1689 Bill of Rights is a historic statute because it takes its place as one of four documents that seeks to regulate the relationship between the Crown and the people.

3 *The Case of Proclamations* [1610] 12 Co Rep 74; 77 ER 1352 – It was stated rather famously that 'the King hath no prerogative, but that which the law of the land allows him.'

The origins of the statute derived following the 'Glorious Revolution,' during King James II's tenure following the death of Charles II. We know that the power of Parliament had grown substantially by this point, and the execution of Charles I in 1649 for high treason was a watershed moment. Despite this, James II, a Roman Catholic (the last Catholic King), went about replacing and appointing other Roman Catholics, repealing penal laws against Roman Catholics, and requesting more money for the Army, which brought him into conflict with Parliament.

Some of the most important declarations that are still valid today can be seen in the operation of Parliament. Articles 8 and 13 provide for the frequent summons of Parliament and free elections, Article 9 provides for MPs and peers to be able to speak freely in Parliament, articles 4 and 6 provide for no taxes to be levied without the prior authority of Parliament and for no armies to be raised in peace time. Finally, and perhaps significantly, articles 1 and 2 state that the consent of Parliament is required in order for any laws to be dispensed with.

1.5.6 The Representation of the Peoples Act 1832, 1867 and 1884

The First Reform Act – the Representation of the Peoples Act 1832 – also known as the Great Reform Act was enacted due to the necessity of parliamentary reform, but to also allow an extension of votes to the growing and influential middle class.

The initial changes (which did not go far enough) sought to reduce some constituencies to 1 MP as well as disenfranchise a number of other boroughs in their entirety. It also sought to create new constituencies, and opened up property qualification in the counties, to now include small landowners, farmers and shopkeepers. Sadly, the Act also excluded women from voting, as the terminology in the Act defined a voter as a male person. The property qualification requirement also meant that the majority of working men still could not vote.

The second Reform Act – Representation of the Peoples Act 1867 – resulted in an increase of voters from approximately 1.4 million to 2.5 million (from a population of 30 million). The property qualification element was extended to renters, meaning that a large-scale increase in voters was seen in many of the newer towns in England and Scotland. The idea was to give the vote to 'respectable working men,' but this still excluded the poor and unskilled workers.

The Third Reform Act – Representation of the Peoples Act 1884 – created further rights for voters. There was a focus on amalgamating the rights of those in the counties and those in the boroughs. The Liberal Party pushed for extension of the voting franchise into rural England, something which did not go down too well with the Conservative Party, as there was a feeling that the party that pushed for their right to vote would gain the votes of those people, and further, it was unlikely that poorer people would vote for a party that was based upon wealth and privilege. The electorate was raised to 5.5 million and was open to all men who rented unfurnished lodgings to the value of £10 a year.

It would not be until the Fifth Reform Act where electoral equality between men and women would be provided, allowing the vote for all women over the age of 21, irrespective of property ownership, which was a prerequisite of the right to vote for women in the Fourth Reform Act. At the time of the Fourth Reform Act, property enfranchisement for men was removed, and women would be allowed to vote subject to being over the age of 30, and occupying premises with a rateable value of £5 (or their spouses did).

1.5.7 European Law from the European Communities Act 1972 through to Assimilated Law

Prior to the UK's admission to the European Union, the European Communities Act 1972 was enacted, which allowed for the UK to enter into the European Economic Community (EEC), from January 1, 1973.

The significance of the Act cannot be understated because in many ways, it affected the notion of Parliamentary Supremacy – given the requirement of the primacy of EU Law over national law. This was done via two mediums.

Firstly, the 1972 Act ensured that some EU laws and treaties would have *direct effect* without Parliament having to pass any legislation to enact the same. The concept of vertical and horizontal direct effect would allow citizens to enforce EU law against a state and each other.

Secondly, some types of EU Legislation would apply to national law once Parliament had adopted it via primary legislation or via secondary legislation. This provided authority to the courts to give precedence to EU Law over national law in cases of conflict.[4]

The Court of Justice of the European Union was a source of law in its own right. The double-barrelled element of EU Law, sovereignty and direct effect meant that EU Law had to take precedence, and judges were under a duty to interpret EU Law in accordance with national law.

To further add to the importance of this, in the event of conflict, citizens were entitled to compensation under the rules of State Liability via the Francovic principles.[5]

4 See Factortame Cases, where the Merchant Shipping Act 1988 was disapplied by the courts for the first time in the UK's constitutional history due to being inconsistent with EU Law. Interim relief was granted, although questions were raised academically about Parliamentary Sovereignty, and whether the disapplication and Parliament's acceptance of constraints on its supremacy had eroded the principle as set by A.V. Dicey.

5 *Andrea Francovich and Others v Italian Republic*, Joined Cases C-6/90 and C-9/90 [1991] ECR I-5357.

EU Law has influenced many areas, including (but not limited to) employment and immigration rights, financial services, the environment, agriculture and trade. It also bestowed upon EU citizens the freedoms to move within the EU (as both workers or citizens) and freedoms to establish themselves in another member state.

Upon the UK's leaving of the European Union, the European Union (Withdrawal) Act 2018 was passed, repealing the European Communities Act 1972. Provisions were made within the Act under sections 2 and 3 that EU Law would continue to have effect in domestic law on and after exit day. The caveat here was that no court or tribunal, as per section 6(1), would be bound by any retained EU Legislation and principles.

The Retained EU Law (Revocation and Reform) Act 2023 has sought to further streamline retained EU Law, by primarily ending the special status of retained EU Law and by restoring primacy and reclaiming Parliamentary Sovereignty. As of 1 January 2024, retained EU law will now be referred to as assimilated law.

1.6 The Civil and Criminal Legal Systems of England and Wales

You are probably familiar with the notion of the English and Welsh system being based heavily around civil law and criminal law.

1.6.1 What is Criminal Law?

Criminal law revolves around those contraventions of law that negatively affect society rather than just one person, although this may well be the case. Parliament enacts laws that confirm what is acceptable and what is not acceptable. A failure to follow such Acts can result in criminal proceedings being brought forth by the Crown Prosecution Service (CPS) and will be heard in the appropriate court based upon its seriousness.

The sanctions/punishment are designed to act as a deterrent.

- **Summary only offences** – or the less serious – are heard in the Magistrates' Court. Some examples of summary only offences are shoplifting (s22A(1) of the Magistrates' Courts Act 1980), driving without insurance (s143 of the Road Traffic Act 1988) and criminal damage where the damage is less than £5000 (s22 of the Magistrates' Courts Act 1980).
- **Indictable only offences** are heard in the Crown Court and are the more serious offences. Some examples of indictable offences are murder (common law), wounding with intent (s18 Offence Against the Persons Act 1861) and rape (s1 of the Sexual Offences Act 2003). It is important to note that for all offences, your client will appear in the Magistrates' Court and enter a plea. The plea will determine the next steps in the case.

- **Either-way offences** are those offences capable of being heard in either the Magistrates' Court or the Crown Court. The decision is made partially by the Magistrate and partially by the defendant. The decision is based around the adequacies of sentencing powers upon conviction (remember, the sentencing power of a Magistrate is six months for a single offence or 12 months for a combination of offences). The second consideration would be one of complexities and any legal issues that may arise that would make in inappropriate to be held in a Magistrate's Court. Remember, the Magistrates are lay personnel.

In the event that a conviction is successful, then a penalty will be sanctioned, appropriate to that set out in sentencing guidelines and legislation. This could be fines, prison sentences or community orders. It is also important to note that defendants must be proven guilty beyond all reasonable doubt.

1.6.2 What is Civil Law?

Civil law is vastly different from criminal law. Its primary concern is dealing with the rights of individuals and property. The development of law now allows for an individual to sue another individual or organisation if it can be proved that a loss has been accrued – whether that is financial, personal or employment/family related. Usually, the end result for such matters is financial compensation (or another equitable remedy).

The law of tort forms part of the civil law. For example, in a claim based on the tort of negligence, the claimant will need to show that the defendant owed them a duty of care, and that such duty was breached because the defendant's behaviour fell below a reasonable standard of care. For example, if an employee suffers an accident at work, a solicitor may be able to show that the injury was caused by failings in the working environment, and subsequently a breach of duty from the employer's perspective. Another example could be landlord and tenant matter, whereby the subject of the relationship is a tenancy agreement between the parties, where obligations have not been fulfilled. Let us say the tenant has not paid rent for more than two months. The landlord can seek possession of the property and the rental arrears in court. In such an instance the judge will hear both parties' submissions and pass a judgment.

It is important to note that unlike criminal law, the burden of proof in these matters is based upon the balance of probability.

1.6.3 Administrative Law

Administrative law, often referred to as public law, is a body of law that seeks to regulate public bodies by holding them to account via the medium of judicial review. It enables the judiciary to ensure the legitimacy of the decisions made by the Executive and by extension, public bodies. Administrative law is not concerned with the merits of a decision – its focus is on the decision-making process, and whether a public body or the Executive has acted *ultra vires* or beyond their powers. The process of judicial review allows an individual to bring to account a governing body if they can demonstrate that a decision made affects them (locus standi) and falls within one of the grounds of judicial review.

An excellent recent example of this working in practice is *R (Miller) v Secretary of State for Exiting the European Union*,[6] whereby it was successfully challenged that the Executive (British Government) could not issue a withdrawal of the UK from the European Union with the use of the Royal Prerogative. This led to the European Union (Notification of Withdrawal) Act 2017.

1.7 The Constitutional Position of the UK

It is often stated that the UK has an unwritten constitution. This statement is not factually correct. It is unwritten in the sense that it has not been codified into a single document that is headed 'Constitution of the United Kingdom.' What we do have, is a collation of documents, *written*, of course, that provide the outlines of a working *uncodified* constitution. It is interesting to note that New Zealand and Israel also do not have codified constitutions.

It is important to think about why this is the case, and the answer is rather obvious.

Many states have codified constitutions due to major state unrest, civil war and granting of independence. If you recall in our discussion for the Bill of Rights at 1.5.5, the last successful civil unrest was the 'glorious' revolution, which, for all intents and purposes, was James I abdicating and William and Mary acceding to the throne. It should be added that there was a very brief constitutional document which was Oliver Cromwell's instrument of government, where he was the Lord Protector.

If we take the UK's position, it is clear to note that when we amalgamate the various sources of documents, we can see a clear allocation of power to and limitations of state power, the preservation of society's fundamental and moral principles and that the country is governed in accordance with democratic principles. The sources of such power can be found in the common law and statutory law such as those mentioned earlier such as the Bill of Rights 1689, Act of Settlement 1701 and Magna Carta 1215, but also Acts such as the Parliament Act 1911 and 1949, the Human Rights Act 1998, the Representation of Peoples Act 2000 and the Constitutional Reform Act 2005.

Statutes that preserve moral principles can be found in the Race Relations Act 1976, the Sex Discrimination Act 1975 and even the Succession to the Crown Act 2013.

6 *R (Miller) v Secretary of State for Exiting the European Union* [2017] UKSC 5.

In addition to the statutes, constitutional conventions play a key role in determining the efficiency of the UK's constitutional position as those working within the constitutional spheres are obliged to follow such conventions.

Thus, the fact that Royal Assent has been granted for all legislation since Queen Anne's withholding of the same in 1708 is a testament to the importance of constitutional conventions. As an example, the convention of ministerial and collective Cabinet responsibility has seen numerous ministers either resign or be dismissed.

Other sources include the Royal Prerogative and prior to 2020, European Union Law. The Royal Prerogative are powers that are exercised by ministers but are powers that are retained by the King or Queen. Some examples of how the Royal Prerogative is utilised can be seen in the way ministers are able to: conduct foreign affairs, negotiating and entering into treaties, declaring war and appointing public officials. The King or Queen utilises their 'reserve' powers under the prerogative by being able to appoint and dismiss a minister, provide Royal Assent to Bills that have been through the legislative process (although it is important to note that Royal Assent will always be given in line with constitutional conventions, as discussed earlier) and summon Parliament (and prorogue Parliament).

Chapter 1 Revision Points

This chapter has provided you with an overview of some of the characteristics of the English Legal System and some of the foundational principles, some of which will be covered in more depth in the following chapters. It is imperative to have a solid understanding of the same, so that you can have a more in depth understanding of the sources of law and statutory interpretation in the next chapter.

It is important to check your knowledge using the following Multiple Choice Questions.

Multiple Choice Questions

Question 1

Jamaal is studying how the legal systems in Wales and England function. He has read about the monarchy's power and how it relates to nobility and the aristocracy. He has also read about the role of the judiciary in terms of decision making and unrest among the public.

Of the following options, which is most accurate?

A. Not the broader public, but the King, the Church of England and the nobility.
B. Not the judiciary, but the broader public, the nobility and the King.
C. Not the trade unions prior to 1800, but the judiciary, the monarchy and the nobility.
D. Not the King, but the nobility, the trade unions and the aristocracy.
E. Not the Church of England, but the judiciary, the nobility and the King.

Question 2

You are a solicitor who works for a firm that specialises in public law. You have been asked by a local school to provide a lecture on the development of the English Legal System and the significance of the UK constitution. Upon the preparation of your talk, you are focussing on Parliament and its role, the rule of law, the European Convention on Human Rights and the significance of the Magna Carta.

Which of the following statements relating to the English Legal System in relation to public law within England and Wales is correct?

A. Decisions made by the European Court of Human Rights must be enacted via legislation in the UK.
B. The rule of law means that aside from those in the Cabinet, everybody else is treated equally.
C. The UK's written and codified constitution has enshrined the Magna Carta.
D. The Government/Executive is the most important institution when thinking about the judiciary, Parliament and the Government.
E. The rule of law states that the law must be applied by judges impartially and without bias.

Question 3

You are a Government Minster working in the Cabinet dealing with an unforeseen event, for which there is no law providing guidance in terms of how to deal with the matter. You do, however, have the full support of the general populace to deal with matter quickly by utilising your powers of the Royal Prerogative, notwithstanding the fact that there is no law surrounding it.

Should you utilise the powers that are granted to you?

A. Yes, because the UK's written constitution allows a government minister to exercise such powers.
B. No, because 'the King has no prerogative but that which the law of the land allows him.'
C. Yes, because the Magna Carta allows use of the Royal Prerogative.
D. No, because you will require Royal Assent, which you may not get.
E. Yes, because if you do not, you will lose the support of the general populace.

PART

2

Sources of Law – Primary Legislation and Statutory Interpretation

2 Primary Legislation

2.1 SQE1 Syllabus

The legislative process, including primary and secondary legislation, the structure of an Act of Parliament and Senedd Cymru.

2.2 Chapter Overview

This chapter will provide an overview of the concept of primary and secondary legislation and their structures, in addition to an overview of the creation of Acts of Parliament, and where the power to create such Acts derives from.

2.3 An Introduction to Parliamentary Sovereignty

Before we delve into the importance of primary legislation, it is perhaps useful for us to cover the principle of Parliamentary Sovereignty, as this will allow you to firstly understand where the power in relation to creating an Act of Parliament derives from.

The supremacy (or sovereignty) of Parliament (or Legislature) is a fundamental principle of the legal system and UK constitution. We saw in our previous chapter how Parliament has evolved and developed over the last millennia, with a significant change after the Bill of Rights 1689. A.V. Dicey summarised the doctrine of Parliamentary Supremacy into three elements. Firstly, Parliament is able to make (and unmake) laws concerning anything; secondly, no Parliament is able to bind itself, its successor or be bound by its predecessors (the rule of the implied repeal); thirdly, no body or court can question the validity of an Act of Parliament (the enrolled Bill rule).

It is important to note that the rule of implied repeal no longer applies to 'constitutional statutes,' which are those that appear to have a higher or more important status than regular Acts of Parliament.[1] As such, statutes can only be

1 See *Lord Justice Laws statement in Thoburn v Sunderland City Council* [2002] EWHC 195 (Admin); [2003] QB 151 at paragraph 62 and 63.

DOI: 10.4324/9781003435525-5

repealed expressly by Parliament. Suggestive constitutional statutes, for example, were outlined as the Bill of Rights 1689, Human Rights Act 1998 and European Communities Act 1972.

Whilst the sovereignty of Parliament is absolute and a fundamental principle of the UK Constitution, they have, over the years, enacted legislation that has limited its authority both in and outside of the UK. These limitations of power revolve around the devolution of power to the Scottish Parliament and the Senedd Cymru; the enacting of the Human Rights Act 1998, by giving effect to the principles of the European Convention on Human Rights into UK Law, enabled courtesy of section 4 of the Act, the possibility of a court declaring a statute incompatible with human rights (and thus questioning its compatibility); entry and exit into the European Union.

2.3.1 The Enrolled Bill Rule

With regards to the validity of primary legislation, it is unquestionable that Acts of Parliament form the highest source of law in the UK. It is important to note that this did differ when membership of the European Union existed, and EU Law asserted supremacy in such matters where national law conflicted with EU Law. In relation to the original point, primary legislation being the highest source of law means that no court or body is able to question the validity of an Act of Parliament. Thus, it is extremely important to understand that a court will not question how primary legislation came into being, but simply have a duty to interpret and apply the legislation using their powers of interpretation.[2]

> All that a Court of Justice can do is to look to the Parliamentary roll: if from that it should appear that a bill has passed both Houses and received the Royal assent, no Court of Justice can inquire into the mode in which it was introduced into Parliament, nor into what was done previous to its introduction, or what passed in Parliament during its various stages through both Houses.[3]
>
> (*Lord Bingham in Jackson and others (Appellants) v Her Majesty's Attorney General (Respondent)* [2005] UKHL 56)

2.3.2 The Implied Repeal Rule

Primary legislation can be amended expressly and impliedly. Going back to our discussion on Parliamentary Sovereignty, it is crucial that if it is to survive, it must be continuing, and accordingly, current Parliaments must have the same power to legislate as previous Parliaments.

2 Even if the creation of the Act itself was based around an allegation of fraud and misleading rationale see *Edinburgh and Dalkeith Railway co v Wauchope* (1842) 8 CL & Fin 710 and *Pickin v British Railways Board* (1974) AC 765.

3 *Edinburgh and Dalkeith Railway Co v Wauchope* (1842) 8 CL & F 710, 725, as quoted by Lord Reid in *Pickin v British Railways Board* (1974) AC 765, and cited in *Jackson and others (Appellants) v Her Majesty's Attorney General (Respondent)* (2005) UKHL 56 at para 27.

Express repeal: When a new Act of Parliament expresses that specific existing statutory rules are abolished.

Implied repeal: Where two statutes provide conflicting rules on the same subject, even where there are no express words, the latest Act impliedly repeals the earlier Act.

For example, let's take a fictitious example of trainee solicitors having to pay a training and qualification levy.

> **The (fictitious) Duty of Trainee Solicitors Act 2023**
>
> Section 1
>
> *all trainee solicitors must contribute £50 per week to a training and qualification levy.*

In order for this to be expressly repealed, a later Act will seek to expressly repeal the Act in question.

> **The (fictitious) Access to Legal Training Act 2024**
>
> Section 1
>
> The (fictitious) Duty of Trainee Solicitors Act 2023 is repealed.

In order for this to be impliedly repealed, a new Act that conflicts with the original Act would be sufficient.

> **The (fictitious) Access to Legal Training Act 2024**
>
> Section 1
>
> Without prejudice to the costs of a higher educational programme, trainee solicitors will not be subject to any other training or qualification levies.

A clear conflict/inconsistency is caused between the 2023 Act where a levy is due, compared to the 2024 Act where no levies are applicable save as to the educational costs.

The final element to consider is that Parliament cannot bind future Parliaments, as that would prohibit them from amending or repealing legislation in the future.[4] The basis of this rule is paramount and fundamental. If the hands of Parliament's

4 See *Vauxhall Estates v Liverpool Corporation* [1932] 1 KB 733 (DC).

law-making ability were tied by a clause in a previous Act of Parliament, then it would show a complete breakdown of the doctrine itself.

> The logical reason why Parliament has failed in its endeavours to enact unchangeable enactments is that a sovereign power cannot, while retaining its sovereign character, restrict its own powers by any parliamentary enactment.

AV Dicey, *Introduction to the Study of the Law of the Constitution* (1898) (10th edn, Macmillan 1959)

2.3.3 Constitutional Statutes

It is important to discuss at this stage the notion of a constitutional statute. Whilst it is fair to state that one Act of Parliament is not anymore 'supreme' than another in terms of importance and hierarchy, this notion is something that simply could not apply to Acts of constitutional significance. We discussed in 2.3 Lord Justice Laws' statement in *Thoburn v Sunderland City Council* [2002] EWHC 195 (Admin), and how certain Acts such as the Human Rights Act 1998, the Act of Union 1707 and the European Communities Act 1972 could not be impliedly repealed like any other Act of Parliament. Whilst in theory, it is simply 'ordinary' primary legislation subject to the supremacy of Parliament, its constitutional importance would render such statutes as anything other than ordinary legislation but deemed to be 'constitutional' legislation. In the Thoburn case (also known as the Metric Martyrs), Lord Justice Laws outlined that a constitutional statute could only be amended or repealed via the use of express language in a later Act of Parliament, which would clearly signify intention of Parliament to alter such legislation. The idea of constitutional statutes as posited by Lord Justice Laws has received support from the Supreme Court in *BH (AP) (Appellant) and another v The Lord Advocate and another (Respondents)* (Scotland) [2012] UKSC 24, in *R (HS2 Action Alliance) v Secretary of State for Transport* [2014] UKSC 3 and also in *R (on the application of Miller and another) v Secretary of State for Exiting the European Union* [2017] UKSC 5.

The element of constitutional statutes has again been discussed with regards to its validity, as the Supreme Court has appeared to apply standard Diceyan Orthodoxy in the recent decision of *Re Allister et al* [2023] UKSC 5, where conflict between the Union with Ireland Act 1800 and Act of Union (Ireland) 1800 (Acts of Union 1800) and the Northern Ireland Protocol to the withdrawal agreement, which was given effect by the European Union Withdrawal Act 2018. The Supreme Court has decided that section 7a of the Act provides for the withdrawal agreement to be given effect in the UK, and any inconsistent legislation (Article VI of the Acts of Union 1800) to be disapplied. The Supreme Court did not assess the concept of Constitutional Statutes as a common law principle.

2.4 What Is Primary Legislation?

As we have already noted, Parliament is able to make or unmake any law as it sees fit, and the legislative process is directly linked to the doctrine of Parliamentary

Sovereignty. They are the institution that are charged with the role of law making, scrutinising Bills and holding the government to account. Accordingly, they are able to create Acts in relation to any element of life in the UK. The Acts can extend and apply to the entire UK territory and nations or local areas. Primary legislation can be described as 'main law' passed by the legislatures within the UK, such as Acts of Parliament, but also those enacted by the Scottish and Welsh Parliaments and Northern Ireland Assembly. You may have seen these types of primary legislation frequently referred to as statutes, the statute book or even statutory law which is a universal term applicable to primary legislation in general.

All primary legislation passed within Parliament must go through a process involving both Houses of Parliament (unless the House of Commons intend to utilise the Parliament Acts) and gaining Royal Assent from the King in Parliament (to be discussed further in 2.4.1). Prior to formally being adopted within the statute book, primary legislation commences as Bills, which are proposals for new laws, which are generally, public, private or hybrid in nature (Table 2.1). Any Bills proposed by the government are public Bills, given they have an impact on the public at large, and are endorsed by the UK Executive.

Table 2.1 Different Bills in Parliament

Type of Bill	Definition	Example
Public Bills	Of general application	Coronavirus Act 2020
Private Bills	Applies to individuals or groups (e.g. local authorities)	Highgate Cemetery Act 2022; Monken Hadley Common Act 2022
Hybrid Bills	Of general application but will affect in a manner different from the general population	High Speed Rail (West Midlands-Crewe) Act 2021; The High-Speed Rail (Crewe-Manchester) Bill is currently before the House of Commons at the Committee Stage[5]
Private Members' Bills	Introduced by an individual MP or peer	Abortion Act 1967, introduced by Liberal MP David Steel; Access to Medical Treatments (Innovation) Act 2016
Government Bills	Introduced by the government	Advanced Research and Invention Agency Act 2022; Anti-social Behaviour, Crime and Policing Act 2014

5 As of 21 August 2023.

Type of Bill	Definition	Example
Money Bills	Contains nothing other than financial matters and is certified as such by the Speaker	Commonwealth Development Corporation Bill 2016-17; Water Industry (Financial Assistance) Bill 2010-12
Consolidation Bill	Re-enactment of existing primary legislation or statutory instruments into one consolidating Act	Road Traffic Act 1998; The Companies Act 2006; Sentencing Act 2020 Consumer Rights Act 2015

Primary legislation can be both criminal and civil, and can also create new law and repeal existing law. It is often the case that Acts are used to rectify issues in substantive areas of law. For example, the Unfair Contract Terms Act 1977 was created in order to rectify some of the issues of the use of unfair terms in contract law. Similarly, the Contracts (Rights of Third Parties) Act 1999 was enacted to assist with creating third party rights in contract beyond the contracting parties and privity of contract. In terms of permanency, primary legislation is permanent, unless repealed by later Acts. Some primary legislation is temporary in nature and will expire based upon information (sunset clause) contained within the Act itself. For example, the London Olympic Games and Paralympic Games Act 2006 had provisions which ceased to have effect at the 'end of the London Olympics Period,' as per section 40(6), and other provisions which ceased to have effect on 31 December 2012, as per section 40(7)(b).

Primary legislation comes into effect once Royal Assent has been received or via another date as specified within the Act.

2.4.1 Creation of Acts of Parliament

As mentioned earlier, all primary legislation starts off in Parliament as a Bill that is to be debated whilst going through a formal enactment process. The dramatis personae within the location in Westminster consists of:

The House of Commons – Lower Chamber

650 MPs chosen via general elections, which must be held by law every five years. MPs play a significant role in debating and making primary legislation by approving Bills that have been proposed by the government.

The House of Lords – Upper Chamber

Around 800 peers including those that are hereditary, and bishops of the Church of England, like the House of Commons, are arranged into political parties, and its role is to consult upon and pass laws and also scrutinise government actions. It has much less power than the House of Commons – but one of its key strengths is its collective wisdom. Life peers were introduced following the enactment of the Life Peerages Act 1958, which resulted in more members from diverse backgrounds representing the House of Lords. In further development, the House of Lords Act 1999 removed the majority of hereditary peers, leaving 91 from 700! The remaining numbers are those of the Lord Spiritual.

The King in Parliament – the Head

Plays a crucial role in providing Royal Assent to Bills that have passed both Houses and go on to become primary legislation. There is no personal gain for the King, his role to provide assent is conventional in nature, and he will always provide assent when asked to do so.

The majority of Bills that are proposed in Parliament are those proposed by the government, given one of the key priorities of the government is to further their mandate and policies.

As Figure 2.1 dictates, the legislative process is extremely structured and commences firstly in the House of Commons, before proceeding to the House of Lords, whereby they will have the same process. Following passage through the House of Lords, the King will grant Royal Assent. It is also important to note that prior to the Royal Assent stage, both Houses must agree on the wording. If the two houses are unable to agree on the wording, the Bill is sent back and forth in what is known as 'Parliamentary Ping Pong,' or consideration of the Lords/Commons amendments. Whilst the House of Lords has the power to send amendments back to the House of Commons for them to further debate, they will avoid attempting to frustrate the House of Commons. Such deliberate acts historically have resulted in the enactment of the Parliament Acts of 1911 and 1949, whereby the House of Commons were able to limit the power of the House of Lords in terms of the outright rejection and the delaying of Bills. These Acts provide Parliament the power to pass certain Acts without requiring the consent of the House of Lords.[6] That said, there are some exclusions with respect to Bills from the Parliament Acts, and accordingly, private Bills, Bills originating from the House of Lords, Bills sent up to the Lords less than a month before the end of a session and Bills extending the life of Parliament beyond five years cannot be passed using the Parliament Acts of 1911 and 1949. Under this method of law making (by overstepping the House of Lords), only seven Bills have become Acts. These are: The Hunting Act 2004, Sexual Offences (Amendment) Act 2000, European Parliament Elections Act 1999, War Crimes Act 1991, Parliament Act 1949, Welsh Church Act 1914 and the Government of Ireland Act 1914.

6 *Jackson and others (Appellants) v Her Majesty's Attorney General (Respondent)* [2005] UKHL 56. There are only seven Bills that have become Acts under this method of law making.

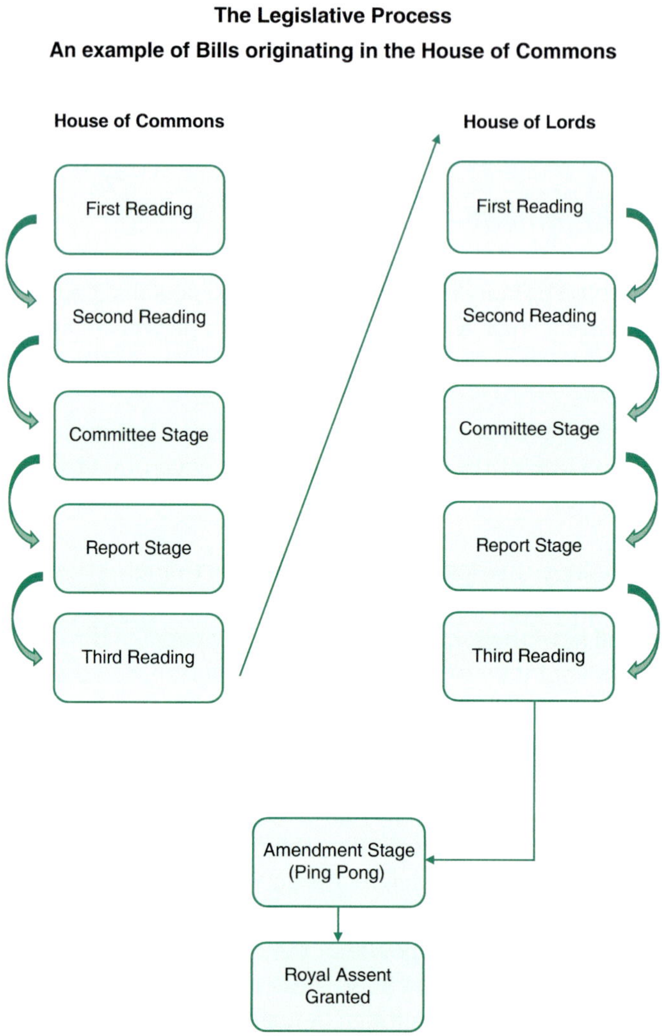

Figure 2.1 The legislative process

2.4.2 The Structure of a Statute

Let's consider the structure of a statute (Figure 2.2).

The Short Title

This appears at the beginning and is the name of the Act – our example is the Hunting Act 2004. You may find it useful to open up the Act to assist you.

Citation and Chapter

This is crucial to ensuring that you are perusing the correct Act. It will also usually appear with a chapter number. In our example, we have 2004, chapter 37. This simply equates to the Act being the 37th Act of 2004.

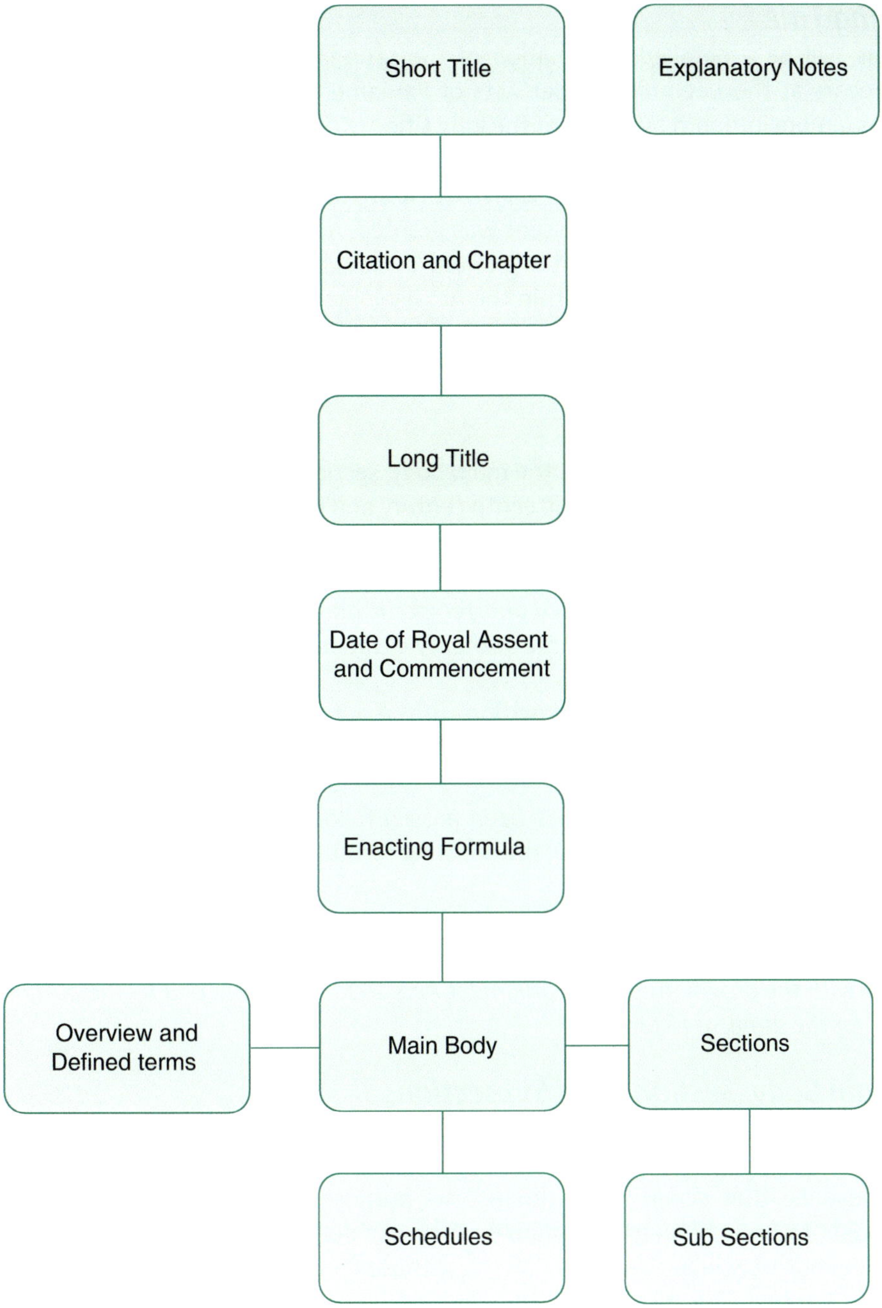

Figure 2.2 The structure of a statute

Long Title

This will be a detailed explanation of the rationale and purpose of the Act. It appears at the beginning. Older Acts of Parliament included a preamble, which was a more in-depth overview of the long title.

Date of Royal Assent and Commencement

This is the date when Royal Assent was granted. An Act may come into force and become law on the day Assent is granted, although it is common for commencement dates to be specified within the Act itself. In our example, per section 15, it states clearly that the Act will come into force at the end of the period after which three months have passed.

Enacting Formula

This is a passage that precedes the main body, sections, and subsections of the Bill. The formula derives from the fifteenth century and is:

> *BE IT ENACTED by the King's most Excellent Majesty, by and with the advice and consent of the Lords Spiritual and Temporal, and Commons, in this present Parliament assembled, and by the authority of the same, as follows:.*

The enacting formula allows provisions of the Act to be introduced which allows for legal effect.

Where an Act of Parliament has been passed following the procedure under the Parliament Acts 1911 and 1949, the enacting formula reads as follows:

> *BE IT ENACTED by The King's most Excellent Majesty, by and with the advice and consent of the Commons in this present Parliament assembled, in accordance with the provisions of the Parliament Acts 1911 and 1949, and by the authority of the same, as follows:*

Main Body, Sections and Subsections

Sections (1, 2, 3, etc.), subsections (1, 2, 3, etc.), paragraphs ((a), (b), and (c)), and subparagraphs ((i), (ii), (iii), etc.) make up an Act's main body. Each section contains a headline that serves to summarise its purpose and may make it easier for readers to find the pertinent clauses. If an Act deals with a variety of topics, its main body may be broken into Parts, and those Parts may then be further divided into Chapters. This also forms the substantive elements of the law that will be relied upon by those seeking to use it.

Schedules

Not all Acts include Schedules, and these are located at the very end. Schedules are used to elaborate on more technical matters, especially if the same would interrupt the flow of the Act in the main body. These are divided in paragraphs and subparagraphs.

Overview

The first section of an Act may sometimes provide an overview of the remainder of the Act in question. This allows the reader to summarise and place into context the Act in question. It is important to note that an overview does not have legal effect – that remains with the individual sections and subsections.

Defined Terms

The vast majority of Acts will also define phrases and words that are crucial to the Act to provide a clear and specific definition. These often can be located in an interpretation section or elsewhere in the Act, but are often also used at the beginning, to allow the user to understand the phrases and provisions.

Explanatory Notes

The purpose of this is to explain the legislation in a user-friendly manner without the need to utilise a legal or other professional. They do not form part of the Act and are not endorsed by Parliament.

2.5 Interpreting an Act of Parliament

Primary legislation is interpreted by the courts when applying the law to cases before them. Judges have a duty to interpret legislation in a manner that gives effect to the will of Parliament. Judges have a duty when interpreting the law to consider the entirety of the text of the Act as a whole and seek to apply the ordinary and natural meaning of the words contained therein.

In cases of ambiguity, a statutory interpretation framework is utilised, whereby judges can consider the Act in detail and draw upon a number of internal and external aids in order to avoid an outcome that is absurd, whilst ensuring the will of Parliament is met.

Some of the common rules that you may come across will be the literal rule, the golden rule, the mischief rule and the purposive approach. These are often used alongside rules of language and construction in order to reach an outcome.

An in-depth coverage of statutory interpretation will be considered in Chapter 3.

2.6 Statutory Instruments and Byelaws

In addition to primary legislation, the legislative process can also be considered in the form of secondary/delegated legislation, which includes statutory instruments and byelaws. The legal authority to make and pass secondary legislation is usually outlined in an enabling Act of Parliament and is usually conferred upon a Minister of the Crown or another body. It is important to note that secondary legislation is subject to judicial review, if it can be shown that a Minister of the Crown or government department has acted *ultra vires* or beyond the power allocated to them via the enabling Act. This marks a stark contrast to primary legislation, as we know that the validity of such statutes will not be questioned by judges.

2.6.1 Statutory Instruments

There are three main types of UK statutory instruments: Orders, Regulations and Rules.

The process in which statutory instruments are made can be found in section 1 of the Statutory Instruments Act 1946, which allows for power conferred on His Majesty, exercisable by Order in Council, and power conferred upon a Minister of the Crown, exercisable by a statutory instrument. Generically speaking, these are merely changes to legislation made by government departments.

On average, there are 3500 statutory instruments that are made every year, of which 1000 may need to be considered by Parliament. They are published with explanatory memorandums, outlining the rationale for the change encompassing either one of rule, regulation or order.

In terms of parliamentary influence, any draft affirmative statutory instruments put before Parliament will require approval via the affirmative procedure. This makes a small percentile of statutory instruments, and the duty to utilise this procedure and request the approval of Parliament (both Houses[7]) is likely to be in the enabling Act. It is important to note that not all statutory instruments require approval by Parliament, and a negative procedure can also be utilised. This allows for a Minster to sign off on the statutory instrument, and then have the same laid in Parliament. This allows for the coming into effect of the change as law, unless Parliament, within a fixed period (usually 40 days), annuls it (prayer motions). The majority of statutory instruments are laid under this procedure.

Statutory instruments can be found on the Parliament website, where statutory instruments can be perused in terms of whether they were part of the negative procedure, or the draft affirmative procedure.

2.6.2 Byelaws

Byelaws are laws created locally, with the authority to create the same deriving from an enabling Act of Parliament. It would be impossible for Parliament to

7 Unless it is a financial matter, for which it would then require just the House of Commons.

legislate for all towns and cities in the UK, especially for matters that are local. Byelaws are enforced locally by local government bodies/councils through the Magistrates' courts. For example, the authority to revoke byelaws, is authorised by section 236b of the Local Government Act 1972.

2.7 Senedd Cymru

The Government of Wales Act 1998 and the Government of Wales Act 2006 created the original Assembly for Wales, which, following the enactment of the Wales Act 2017, has since been renamed Senedd Cymru after insertion of section A1 into the Government of Wales Act 2006. Section A2, again as inserted by the Wales Act 2017 into the Government of Wales Act 2006 creates legislative authority for Welsh Law that is created by Senedd Cymru. These powers are derived from S108A and Schedule 7A and B as stipulated within the Government of Wales Act 2006.

You may have seen Senedd Cymru also referred to as the Welsh Parliament. Its duty is to utilise the devolved power as authorised by Parliament in Westminster to create laws for Wales respectively.

Senedd is able to pass Acts of Senedd, which is primary legislation. This takes a slightly different process to Westminster Acts of Parliaments, as detailed later. These Bills once they have passed through the process will receive Royal Assent, thus becoming enforceable Acts of Senedd.

2.7.1 The Legislative Process (Senedd Cymru)

Figure 2.3 provides an overview of Bills and the process that they must proceed through prior to becoming an Act of Senedd. Bills are usually proposed by the Welsh Government or by members via a Member's Bill. Private Bills can also be submitted, although this is somewhat rare. Once the Bill in question has reached stage 4 successfully and is approved by Senedd, then it will receive Royal Assent from the monarch, and become an Act.

It is important to note that these powers have been conferred upon Senedd by the Westminster Parliament via devolution. The initial Government of Wales Act created a Welsh Government and the Welsh Assembly, via a conferred powers system, whereby the limits of power was outlined in the enabling Act of Parliament.

Devolution of power to Scotland, Wales and Northern Ireland forms an important cornerstone of the legal system.

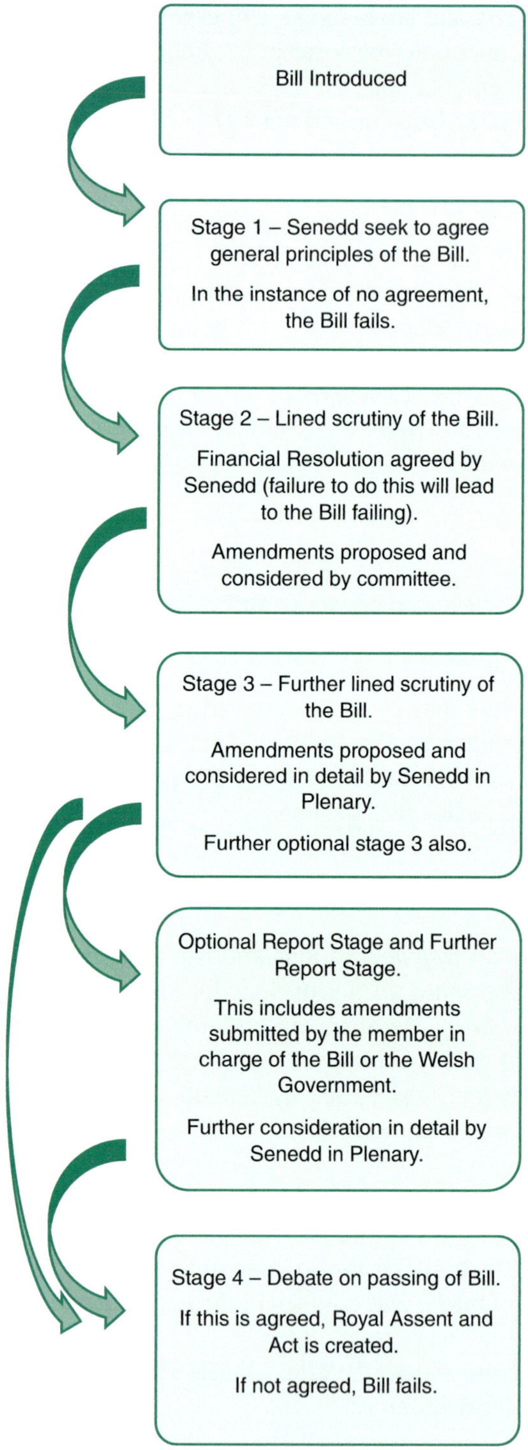

Figure 2.3 An overview and the process of Bills

Chapter 2 Revision Points

With this chapter, we have considered some key areas of understanding required for SQE1, namely the consideration of primary legislation and structure of an Act of Parliament. We have also taken the time to consider the powers and procedures for the enactment and implementation of both primary and secondary legislation, and how such legislation may also be repealed.

- Parliament is the supreme law-making body in the United Kingdom.
- Primary legislation is the highest source of law in the United Kingdom.
- A court will not question the validity of an Act of Parliament.
- The doctrine of Parliamentary Supremacy means Parliament can make and unmake any law and cannot bind future Parliaments.
- Primary legislation commences as a proposal (Bill) and must be passed by both houses before receiving Royal Assent.
- Some laws passed under the Parliament Acts 1911 and 1949 can avoid the House of Lords in the enactment process.

It is important to check your knowledge using the following Multiple Choice Questions.

Multiple Choice Questions

Question 1

The (fictitious) Land and Property Act 2024 has proceeded through Parliament and is now at the 'ping pong' stage. Given the changes that it is proposing to the area of land law, it is a substantial piece of legislation, with multiple sections and significant interest in both Houses.

In terms of the legislative process, when will the Bill become an Act?

A. At the Report Stage in the Commons.
B. At the Committee Stage in the Lords.
C. On Royal Assent.
D. At the Third Reading in the Lords.
E. At the Third Reading in the Commons.

Question 2

Parliament is seeking to repeal the (fictional) Acquisition of Land Act 2000 with a new piece of legislation the (fictional) Acquisition of Housing Act 2024.

Which of the following is most likely to apply?

A. Parliament can pass the (fictional) Acquisition of Housing Act 2024 and if it conflicts with the (fictional) Acquisition of Land Act 2000 that is clearly inconsistent with the previous Act, then this will suffice.
B. The Constitution requires all Acts of Parliament to be expressly repealed as otherwise, this would cause uncertainty.
C. Parliament must have a statement in the Act that clearly states that the (fictional) Acquisition of Housing Act 2024 was repealing the (fictional) Acquisition of Land Act 2000.
D. Parliament will first require the (fictional) Acquisition of Land Act 2000 to be formally repealed, and *then* enact the (fictional) Acquisition of Housing Act 2024.
E. Parliament will first have to ask the Supreme Court to disapply the (fictional) Acquisition of Land Act 2000, and then they will be able to enact the (fictional) Acquisition of Housing Act 2024.

Question 3

As a constituent has written to your local Member of Parliament (MP) regarding the (fictitious) Land and Property Act 2023. Your local MP (whose party is not in government) will be taking part in contributing to the development of this Bill.

Which of following ways will your local MP be able to contribute?

A. They can make a speech, as an MP, during the Third Reading of the Bill in the House of Lords.
B. They can speak, as an MP, in a meeting at Cabinet.
C. They can vote, as an MP, in the House of Lords as a peer.
D. They can vote, as an MP, in the House of Lords as a hereditary peer.
E. They can vote, as an MP, in the House of Commons at the Second Reading.

PART 3 Statutory Interpretation

3 Statutory Interpretation

3.1 SQE1 Syllabus

Statutory interpretation: Literal rule, golden rule, mischief rule, purposive approach, presumptions, aids to statutory interpretation and construction.

3.2 Chapter Overview

Now that we have considered the legislative process in relation to the creation of primary legislation, this chapter will now seek to delve into how legislation is interpreted by the courts, with the use of a structured interpretation framework. This framework is based around the use of clear rules of interpretation and construction.

3.3 Divining Parliamentary Intention – The Statutory Interpretation Framework

Statutory interpretation is the process whereby a court is able to identify the meaning of words that may be ambiguous in a statute and apply them to the case at hand before them.

Statutory interpretation is essential to the English Legal System, as it works hand in hand with judicial precedent, and affirmation by the courts to the sovereignty of Parliament, by applying and respecting the will of Parliament and their intentions when a statute was created. The court has a duty to ascertain the objective intention of Parliament.[1]

There are many reasons as to why statutory interpretation (Figure 3.1) is necessary, but often, they are based upon:

- Use of broad terminology by Parliament, for example, 'vehicle,' 'type,' 'animal.'
- Ambiguity in words that could have two or three different meanings.

1 *Pepper v Hart* [1993] AC 593.

DOI: 10.4324/9781003435525-7

- Statutes may be drafted deliberately in a vague manner, for example the Equality Act 2010, where any 'religious or philosophical belief' is a protected characteristic.
- It is impossible for statutes to be drafted in a manner that covers for every possible eventuality.
- Due to human nature, parliamentary drafts-people may have drafted an Act that was complicated, obscure or simply poorly executed.

3.4 Statutory Interpretation Rules

There is a presumption in the common law that when primary legislation is enacted, the passing of such a law is based upon the clear intentions of Parliament with regards to the content of the law in question, and thus should also be interpreted alike.

Accordingly, the framework sets rules and guidance that must be followed, with the outcome of any decision based upon the legislature's intention to create the statute in the first instance. As we will see, in the event that there are issues with regards to interpretation of the law, judges will be able to evaluate and apply the most appropriate interpretation to the specific situation.

The role of a court, and by extension, a judge, is to understand and apply the law to a specific problem (or mischief) that a law has been created to resolve. As such, the court must also be aware of any pre-existing laws, and if those laws still exist, and the necessity of passing the law in question.

To that end, a wealth of pre-enactment information could be available to the courts to ensure and understand what the necessity and justification for a specific law was, and more importantly, the mischief it was created to resolve.

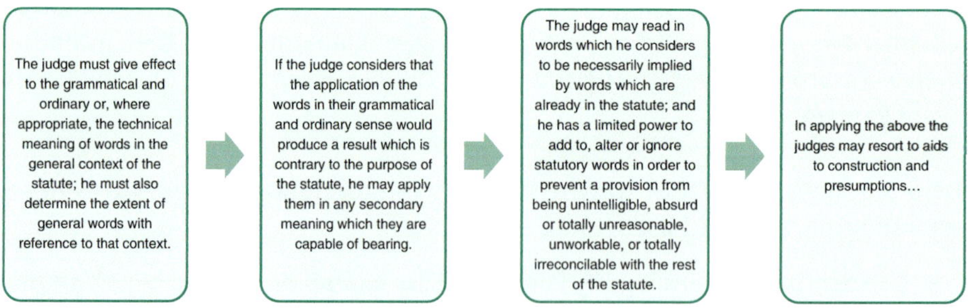

Figure 3.1 Statutory interpretation process

Source: J Bell and G Engle, *Cross on Statutory Interpretation* (3rd Edition, Butterworths, 1995).

Prior to the enactment of any legislation, it is well known that committees are created to research an existing problem, which will allow a foundation to propose new legislation or propose alterations to existing legislation. You may have already come across some of these committees, by way of parliamentary select committees and law commission proposals. These reports are deemed to be part of the pre-enactment history and can be used as an aid to interpret statutes.

For example, we previously mentioned in Chapter 2 at 2.4 that the Contracts (Rights of Third Parties) Act 1999 was enacted to assist with creating third party rights in contract beyond the contracting parties and privity of contract. The foundation of this law and justification of the Act in question was based upon a Law Commission report – *Privity of Contract: Contracts for the Benefit of Third Parties*: Law Com. No. 242, published on 31 July 1996 – drafted by Professor Andrew Burrows, who was Law Commissioner for England and Wales, and Professor of English Law. The Act itself is supported by explanatory notes that include an introduction, summary, background and commentary regarding the Act and its provisions. The background of the explanatory notes cites the law commission report as a basis of the Act's implementation. The explanatory notes are included routinely as part of a Bill and allow judges to be able to refer to the same as an interpretative aid.

Furthermore, the enactment history is also of importance following the ruling in *Pepper v Hart* [1993] AC 593, which we will review in more depth at 3.7.3. However, it is important to note that the decision allows judges to utilise Hansard to assist with interpretation of the law, by considering statements made by the promoter of the Bill. Prior to this, the exclusionary rule did not permit judges to use anything other than the Act itself to come to decisions.

When dealing with any Act, the courts have a duty to interpret its meaning in a manner that allows it to be applied to the facts of the case before them. As such, the courts have been able to develop some rules of interpretation to assist them. As mentioned earlier, judges must consider the purpose of the legislation and Parliament's intention in creating the same.

In addition, Acts must be read by judges in their entirety to ensure that a consistent level of interpretation takes place.[2] There is further development of this in 3.5.

2 *R(O (A Child) v Secretary of State for Home Department* [2022] UKSC 3.

Per Lord Hodge at 29 'Words and passages in a statute derive their meaning from their context. A phrase or a passage must be read in the context of the section as a whole and in the wiser context of a relevant group of sections. Other provisions in a statute and the statute as a whole may provide the relevant context. They are the words which Parliament has chosen to enact as an expression of the purpose of the legislation and are therefore the primary source by which meaning is ascertained.'

3.4.1 The Literal Rule

The literal rule, by its very nature, is to interpret the words of an Act in the literal sense, that is to say, that a judge will look at the Act in the normal sense, grammatically and syntactically. This method is based on the notion that by interpreting the words literally, the will of Parliament is being given effect, even if it may lead to an absurd result.

The case of *Fisher v Bell* [1961] 1 QB 394 is an excellent example of the use of this rule.

The displaying by Mr James Charles Bell of a flick knife in a shop window was deemed by George Fisher, Chief Inspector, as 'an offer for sale' contravening section 1 of the Restriction of Offensive Weapons Act 1959 and was duly prosecuted. During his trial, the judges came to the conclusion that as per established contract law, an 'offer for sale' was not the same as 'invitation to treat.' That is to say, any potential purchaser would be invited to make an 'offer' and it would be sold, but as per the law of the land (at the time), it was clear that the terminology 'offer for sale,' was not an offer capable of acceptance. Furthermore, Lord Parker CJ made it clear that Parliament in creating the law, must have known that to be the case. He further stated that other Acts had words that would otherwise have covered the contravention, such as 'offering or exposing for sale.' He also noted that in other statutes – such as the Prices of Goods Act 1939 and the Goods and Services (Price Control) Act 1941 – when Parliament wished to enlarge the meaning of words, they included a definition section. He also elaborated further:

> at first sight it sounds absurd that knives of this sort cannot be manufactured, sold, hired, lent, or given, but apparently they can be displayed in shop windows; but even if this – and I am by no means saying it is – is a casus omissus it is not for this court to supply the omission.

Needless to say, this 'loophole' in the law was remedied very quickly, with the use of the words to 'expose or to have in their possession for the purpose of sale or hire.'

The case of *Partridge v Crittenden* (1968) 2 All ER 421 followed a similar factual matrix as *Fisher v Bell* and resulted in an advertisement offering for sale bramble finch birds in contravention of section 5 of the Protection of Birds Act 1954, resulting in the overturning of the conviction when applying the literal rule of interpretation on appeal. Again, the terminology of the Act contained the phrase 'offer for sale' which was merely an 'invitation to treat' and interpreting it any other way would appropriate Parliament's intentions, given they had created the Act based upon their understanding, and to alter the same was not the role of the court.

Clearly, the use of the literal rule ensures on the one hand that Parliamentary Sovereignty is respected. However, it is also fair to say that Parliament in drafting the Act in question would never have intended an absurd result. This can be seen in the interesting case of *Whiteley v Chappel* (1868) LR 4 QB 147. It is also important to note that words are imperfect and carry more than one meaning.

3.4.2 The Golden Rule

The golden rule of statutory interpretation may come into effect whereby the literal rule as discussed in 3.4.1 leads to an absurd result that Parliament could not have intended. It is important to note that in such a situation, ordinary words require ordinary meanings and technical words technical meanings. In this instance, the judge may substitute a reasonable meaning when construing the statute as a whole.

The case of *Adler v George* [1964] 1 All ER 62 is an excellent example of the use of this rule.

Section 3 of the Official Secrets Act 1920 provided that

> No person in the *vicinity of any prohibited place* shall obstruct, knowingly mislead or otherwise interfere with or impede, the chief officer or a superintendent or other officer of police, or any member of His Majesty's forces engaged on guard, sentry, patrol, or other similar duty in relation to the prohibited place, and, if any person acts in contravention of, or fails to comply with, this provision, he shall be guilty of a misdemeanour (emphasis added).

The defendant was a protester who managed to gain access to an RAF base, whereby he staged his protest and obstructed a member of Her Majesty's Royal Air Force.

The defendant argued that if he was on the RAF base (which he was) then he could not be in the vicinity of the RAF Base, and accordingly, unless he was in the vicinity, (in the normal sense of the word near to), then the section would not be applicable to his matter. This would be the case if the statute was interpreted in the literal sense. This was important, as while he still committed an offence by obstructing an officer, he would have been indicted under an Act that contained a much more lenient penalty.

However, in this instance, in dismissing his appeal, the court felt anything otherwise would result in an absurdity, if a perpetrator could be found indictable for an offence that takes place in the vicinity of the RAF base, but no offence was created if the obstruction took place inside the RAF base itself. As such, the meaning of 'vicinity' was applied to mean 'in or in the vicinity of,' which results in no violence to the language of the Act itself, and corrected quite clearly what would have been a result that would otherwise have been deemed wholly illogical and impracticable.

The use of this rule allows an absurdity to be prevented if the courts had opted to use the literal rule.

3.4.3 The Mischief Rule

The mischief rule of statutory interpretation was laid down in *Heydon's Case* (1584) 3 Co Rep 7 in the sixteenth century. There are four elements that judges must consider prior to using the same:

1) What was the common law before the making of the Act?
2) What was the mischief and defect for which the common law did not provide?
3) What remedy the parliament hath resolved and appointed to cure the diseases of the commonwealth; and
4) The true reason for the remedy; and then the office of all the judges is always to make such construction as shall suppress the mischief.

The case of *Smith v Hughes* [1960] 1 WLR 830 is an excellent example of the use of this rule.

The Street Offences Act 1959 made it illegal for people to loiter or solicit themselves in the street for the purpose of prostitution. Section 1 stated: 'It shall be an offence for a common prostitute to loiter or solicit in a street or public place for the purpose of prostitution.'[3]

Accordingly, to circumvent the legal issues of loitering and soliciting in the street, the defendants solicited from a first-floor balcony, by drawing the attention of would-be customers, and then invited them in, by indicating the door to the premises.

It was submitted by the defendants that the first-floor balcony was not technically in the street, within the meaning of section 1 of the Act, and as such, no offences could have been committed.

The court opted to consider what the mischief was aimed at by the Act, and this was because a literal interpretation of the rules would clearly have resulted in no offence. The Act was created to prohibit prostitution in the street (the mischief), and it did not matter whether that was done in the street or the doorway of a building, or balcony or window, as in each case (there were six!), all had resulted in an attempt to solicit, and these solicitations were addressed to somebody walking by.

The advantage of this rule again shows how it can avoid an illogical decision, but by way of criticism, the three considerations established by *Heydon's Case* were in

3 The current version now states: It shall be an offence for a [person] [aged 18 or over] (whether male or female) [persistently] to loiter or solicit in a street or public place for the purpose of prostitution.

a period when statutes were a minor source of law, and drafting was not as precise as it now is.

3.4.4 The Purposive Approach

Using the literal rule in statutory interpretation was to focus on the literal meaning of the words, and this often would result in somewhat absurd or illogical outcomes. The purposive approach has European Community jurisprudence and focusses on giving effect to the purpose of an Act or law. That is to say, the courts are seeking to achieve what Parliament's intentions were – the 'purpose of the law.' As such, by giving effect to the true purpose of the law, if needs be, the courts may linguistically strain the meaning of legislation.

The case of *R v Secretary of State for Health ex parte Quintavalle (on behalf of Pro-Life Alliance)* 2003 UKHL 13 is an excellent example of the use of this rule.

The Human Fertilisation and Embryology Act 1990 was created to outlaw and control practices relating to the use of human embryos. When the Act was passed, embryos could only be created by use of a fertilisation method with sperm. Scientific and technological developments in the area resulted in a new method of embryo creation called cell nuclear replacement (CNR).

The applicant, acting via the pressure group, Pro-Life, submitted that due to CNR being a novel method, it was not subject to the 1990 Act, and as such, research under the 1990 Act could not be licensed by the Human Fertilisation and Embryo Authority. Their submission was based upon section 1 of the Act defining an embryo as 'a live human embryo where fertilisation is complete' and that CNR does not involve a process of fertilisation. Accordingly, the licensing of such CNR embryos was prohibited by section 3 of the Act.

> The court's task, within the permissible bounds of interpretation, is to give effect to Parliament's purpose. So, the controversial provisions should be read in the context of the statute as a whole, and the statute as a whole should be read in the historical context of the situation which led to its enactment.
>
> (Lord Bingham, *R v Secretary of State for Health ex parte Quintavalle (on behalf of Pro-Life Alliance)* 2003 UKHL 13)[4]

The use of this approach is now a legitimate interpretative method. It allows, on the one hand an opportunity for judges to take a more creative approach to interpretation to implement the legislature's intentions and purpose of the Act itself. On the other, there is an argument that judges could be acting as de facto law makers, if they attempt to decide what Parliament intended when enacting the legislation in the first instance.

4 Paragraph 8.

3.4.5 The Interaction of the Rules

The basic approach to statutory interpretation is that it can be described as an art, and not a science. As Mann J asserted in *Adobe Systems Inc v Netcom Distributors* [2012] EWHC 1087 (Ch) 'one man's distortion is another man's interpretation.'[5]

Furthermore, in *Maunsell v Olins* [1975] AC 373 HL, Lord Reid went on to state that 'rules of construction are . . . not rules in the ordinary sense of having some binding force. They are our servants, not our masters.'[6]

The rules that we have discussed are designed to aid judges in reaching decisions that will not result in absurdities, or an illogical outcome. The will and intention of Parliament is the pre-eminent criteria which underpin the construction of any statute. Accordingly, the criteria of each of the methods of interpretation that we have discussed all provide their own criteria and rules, and in the event that interpretation is required, judges will apply the most appropriate method of interpretation. There is no preference as to interpretation and that in itself is a limiting factor.

There are, however, some other clear inherent criticisms that present themselves with this manner of interpretation. The literal rule has often been criticised as by placing an emphasis on the literal meaning of words, it presupposes that a draftsperson has the freedom to choose which words they will use in the Act, and the same leaves no room for a difference of opinion as to its meaning. The approach often can lead to absurd results and no solutions – especially if a judge is seeking to apply the rule.

The golden rule also carries criticisms, in the sense that its existence is based upon the negative standard of absurdity, inconsistency or inconvenience. It is important to note that one of the key critiques of the rule is the fact that the concept of absurdity is not means tested.

The English approach entails less of a choice between opposing rules and more of a progressive analysis in which the judge first considers the ordinary meaning of the words in the overall context of the statute – a broad view of what constitutes the 'context' is taken – and then moves on to consider other possibilities in cases where the ordinary meaning results in an absurd outcome.[7]

3.5 Rules of Language and Construction

In addition to the rules of interpretation discussed, further aids have been developed in the common law to help with statutory interpretation. The rules of language (also referred to as canons of construction and linguistic presumptions) are crucial when discussing statutory interpretation, as they serve as a guide in understanding the

5 *Adobe Systems Inc v Netcom Distributors* [2012] EWHC 1087 (Ch), 14.
6 *Maunsell v Olins* [1975] AC 373, 382.
7 J Bell and G Engle, *Cross on Statutory Interpretation* (3rd edition Butterworths, 1995).

meaning of words. Ambiguity is a common theme that judges face when interpreting statutes, and the rule of language plays a very important role. As discussed, Acts must be read in their entirety, as this will enable any inconsistencies to be avoided, by keeping the terminology and wording in the Act in perspective.

The maxims that follow are devices which aid judges in working out the definition of a word depending on its placement within the sentence structure. These rules arise not from law, but from rules of grammar and syntax.

3.5.1 Noscitur a Sociis

The first rule of language to consider is the noscitur a sociis, which can be loosely translated to 'a word draws meaning from those around it' or 'it is known by its associates.' The principle here is that when a word has an ambiguous or uncertain meaning, the word should be construed in light of the words that surround it. Thus, it is not so much the meaning of a single uncertain word, but what that word means when interpreted by construing those that surround it.

> English words derive colour from those which surround them. Sentences are not mere collections of words to be taken out of the sentence, defined separately by reference to the dictionary of decided cases, and then put back into the sentence with the meaning which you have assigned to them as separate words.
>
> *Bourne (Inspector of Taxes) v Norwich Crematorium Ltd* [1967] 1 WLR (QB) 696
>
> See also *Foster v Diphwys Casson Slate Co* (1887) 18 QBD 428.

3.5.2 Ejusdem Generis

We move on to the next maxim, which is ejusdem generis. This can be loosely translated to 'of the same type.' Here, a generic term utilised in a list consisting otherwise of specific words or items takes its meaning from those words or items. For example, '[term] includes A, B and C and other things.' For an example like this, generic words such as 'other things' must be interpreted consistently with the common characteristics of A, B and C.

A common issue that will also apply to noscitur a sociis is when ejusdem generis is applicable, words will be restricted by implication from other words in the list. That is to say, when general words are listed with restrictive words, the rule will seek to restrict those general words alongside the more restrictive one.

In *R v Uddin* [2017] EWCA Crim 1072, the Court of Appeal considered whether the words 'or otherwise' in the definition of a 'vulnerable adult' as per section 5(6) of the Domestic Violence, Crime and Victims Act 2004 could be interpreted to include a category of vulnerable adult who were not suffering from 'illness, disability or old age.' The respondent's submission that the maxim ejusdem generis apply, as 'or otherwise' should be construed in light of the preceding words, which were 'physical, or mental disability or illness, through old age' was rejected.[8]

See also *Richardson v DPP* [2019] 4 WLR 46.

3.5.3 Expressio Unius est Exclusio Alterius

The next tool to consider is expressio unius est exclusio alterius which can be loosely translated to 'the inclusion of one suggests the exclusion of others.' Here, we can further elaborate to if a list expressly mentions a specific item, but does not include similar items, it can be assumed that the intention was only to include the expressly mentioned item. That is to say, the express inclusion of one suggests the exclusion of others.

It should be noted that this maxim has faced criticism from the judiciary. The rigidity of the rule may lead to unfair and unjust outcomes due to the exclusion of other items. This also leaves no scope for development of the law.

3.5.4 Application of the Language Rules

The rules of language also have a common-sense approach to rules of construction. In the event that there are two opposing interpretations of an Act, the judges should prefer the maxim that is most appropriate in terms of common sense, and the **objective** intentions of Parliament are being met.

3.6 Legal Presumptions

When judges interpret legislation, there is also a reliance on a number of presumptions. In this sense, it is the case that these presumptions are already implied within the statute that they are interpreting. These legal presumptions may be rebutted by clear wording, if Parliament's intention is contrary to such presumptions.

Some examples are listed:

> **Parliament is presumed to not legislate extraterritorially.**
>
> Unless clearly express or inferred from language, Parliament does not enact statutes that are to operate beyond the territorial limits of the United Kingdom.
>
> See *Serco v Lawson* [2006] ICR 250 (HL).[9]

8 Per paragraph 35 of the judgment

> we reject the submission that the words or otherwise should be construed ejusdem generis so that or otherwise becomes similar to those listed. Section 5(6) does not justify such an interpretation. It does not for instance say 'some other similar reason' or 'some like reason' or 'some equivalent reason' or 'a reason of a similar type.' If Parliament had wished to link 'other reason' to the identified categories, then it could easily have chosen any of these drafting techniques. It did not do so.

9 Per Lord Hoffman, 'The general principle of construction is, of course, that legislation is prima facie territorial. The United Kingdom rarely purports to legislate for the whole world.'

Parliament is presumed not to legislate retrospectively.

The presumption here is clear in the sense that any Act that alters the law has effect prospectively and not retrospectively. This, however, can be rebutted should Parliament's intention expressly state otherwise. In statutes involving criminal law and tax, the likelihood of retrospective law is not possible, simply because society is expected to regulate their conduct knowing what the law is.

See *The Boucraa* [1994] 1 AC 486 (HL) 525.[10]

Parliament is presumed to not impose burdens or remove rights in the absence of clear wording.

When changes to the law are made, these should be measured and deliberate. We looked at the process for enacting statutes, and the process for the same is measured. However, in the event that well established laws and, including common law, are to be altered, then there is a presumption that this will be done expressly and unambiguously.

See *National Assistance Board v Wilkinson* [1952] 2 QB 648[11]

Presumption to not oust the jurisdiction of the courts.

Notwithstanding the doctrine of Parliamentary Sovereignty, the courts will not accept any legislative attempts to control or oust their jurisdiction. The use of 'ouster clauses' in legislation will be strictly interpreted.[12]

See *Anisminic Ltd v Foreign Compensation Commission* [1969] 2 AC 147.[13]

3.7 Aids to Interpretation

To avoid judges exercising their duty to interpret in a manner that could be classed as inconsistent, or even in part, rules of interpretation governed by both a common law and statutory duty have been created.

10 Per Lord Mustill 'My Lords, it would be impossible now to doubt that the court is required to approach questions of statutory interpretation with a disposition, and in some cases a very strong disposition, to assume that a statute is not intended to have retrospective effect.'

11 Per Lord Goddard CJ, 'It is a well-established principle of construction that a statute is not to be taken as effecting a fundamental alteration in the general law unless it uses words that point unmistakably to that conclusion.'

12 *Per Lord Reid in Anisminic Ltd v Foreign Compensation Commission* [1969] 2 AC 147, 'It is a well-established principle that a provision ousting the ordinary jurisdiction of the court must be construed strictly – meaning, I think, that, if such a provision is reasonably capable of having two meanings, that meaning shall be taken which preserves the ordinary jurisdiction of the court.'

13 The clause in question was section 4(4) of the Foreign Compensation Act 1950 – 'The determination by the commission of any application made to them under this Act shall not be called in question in any court of law.'

3.7.1 Internal Aids

Along with the consideration of the rules of language and cannons of constructions, internal aids are aids that can be utilised which are usually connected to the statute itself. **Remember, the Act has to be interpreted in its entirety.**

In Chapter 2 we considered the legislative process, and the discussion and structure of a statute at 2.4.2 will assist here.

To that effect, judges can refer to:

- **The long title**: These are small introductory statements that do not offer much interpretative guidance to a judge.
- **The short title**: Like the preceding, are limited in their use.
- **The preamble**: This also could be a useful interpretative tool as it provides the rational for enacting the law, however, judges will prefer the main sections and subsections of the Act.
- **Headings before sections**: These can be an interpretative aid as they indicate the rationale and focus of the following parts.
- **References to other enactments in the Act:** These can provide context for judges and such Acts can be used as an interpretative guide.
- **Schedules of the Act:** These provide crucial information and so can be used as an interpretative guide.
- **Sections:** These explain the will of Parliament and outline what the law is.

It is important to note that the listed internal aids are used in addition to the pre-discussed rules of language and the presumptions.

3.7.2 External Aids

We touched briefly upon some of these external aids in 2.5.

External aids, by comparison, are aids that are found 'outside' of the statute. Like 3.7.1 earlier, judges may refer to additional sources that will aid their interpretation but will play a secondary role. It is important to note that they do not displace the meaning conveyed by the actual words of the statute if they are clear and unambiguous.[14]

- **Pre-enactment history**: As discussed earlier in 2.4, the pre-enactment history of the Act can act as an interpretative aid, as it will allow a judge to consider the context and why Parliament has legislated in the area.
- **Explanatory notes**: These can be used as an interpretive aid as they provide the court with the contextual scene of the statute and the mischief it is aimed at.
  Exceptionally, the explanatory notes could prevent the Executive from arguing contrary interpretation.

14 *R(O (A Child) v Secretary of State for Home Department* [2022] UKSC 3.

- **Dictionaries and textbooks**: These are often used for statutory interpretation purposes as it allows a judge to ascertain the meaning of a word. It is routine for a court to have access to an Oxford English Dictionary, if an aid to interpretation of a word is required.
- **Pre-legislation reports**: As part of the pre-enactment history, reports are drafted that seek to outline the mischief the proposed law is seeking to address. Prior to the enactment of any legislation, it is well known that committees are created to research an existing problem, that will allow a foundation to propose new legislation or propose alterations to existing legislation. Often, parliamentary select committees and law commission proposals, in addition to royal commissions create reports that are deemed to be part of the pre-enactment history and can be used as an aid to interpret statutes.

  There is a suggestion that these are only acceptable for use if attempting to determine mischief. See *Fothergill v Monarch Airlines Ltd* [1981] AC 251.[15]
- **International treaties**: Treaties and international conventions can be considered in conjunction with the presumption that Parliament does not legislate in a manner that would be in breach of its international obligations. As such, materials could be utilised to determine the purpose of the statute and were heavily utilised during the UK's membership of the EU.
- **The Interpretation Act 1978**: This Act can also be used as an interpretative aid as it provides presumptions as to people, gender and relationships. For example, if a statute refers to a person as 'he' that will also mean 'she.' As we move into a more gender-neutral society, this will be reflected in the Act in the future.
- **Hansard**: Generally speaking, parliamentary debates cannot be consulted to derive the intention of Parliament.[16] However, judges are now frequently referring to extraneous material used during the legislative process. This is because of the rule enunciated in *Pepper v Hart* [1993] AC 593.

3.7.3 *Pepper v Hart* [1993] AC 593

In the case of *Pepper v Hart* [1993] AC 593, it was established that parliamentary debates may be consulted where:

a) The legislation is ambiguous or obscure or leads to an absurdity.
b) The material relied on consists of one or more statements by a minister or other promoter of the Bill together, if necessary, with such other parliamentary material as is necessary to understand such statements and their effect.
c) The statements relied on are clear.

15 Per Lord Diplock 'Where the Act has been preceded by the report of some official commission or committee that has been laid before Parliament and the legalisation is introduced in consequence of that report, the report itself may be looked at in court for the limited purpose of identifying the "mischief" that the Act was intended to remedy.'

16 *Beswick v Beswick* [1968] AC 58 per Lord Reid, 'For purely practical reasons, we do not permit debates in either House to be cited.'

There is, however, a need for caution. See *Robinson v Secretary of State for Northern Ireland* [2002] UKHL 32.

In *Wilson v Secretary of State for Trade and Industry* [2003] UKHL 40 the courts further elaborated on the use of Hansard in matters whereby the subjective opinions of individual ministers should not be utilised as a means to measure the will of Parliament.[17]

Chapter 3 Revision Points

- Judges are required to interpret the laws created by Parliament with the use of a structured interpretation framework.
- Statutory interpretation must give effect to the will of Parliament. Judges are unable to interpret otherwise.
- In cases of ambiguity, judges can draw upon a number of internal and external aids to avoid an absurd outcome.
- Judges must firstly consider the Act in its entirety in order to determine legislative intent and the purpose of the Act.
- In cases of ambiguity, rules such as the literal rule, golden rule, mischief rule and purposive approach are commonly utilised in order to interpret statutes. Currently, the purposive approach is preferred.
- The court can also draw upon maxims and presumptions in order to determine legislative intent when an ambiguity presents itself.
- Judges can also draw upon external aids, such as Hansard, following the decision in *Pepper v Hart* to again, interpret and understand the wider context of the Act in question.

It is important to check your knowledge using the following Multiple Choice Questions.

17 Per Lord Nicholls at para 67 – 'Beyond this use of Hansard as a source of background information, the content of parliamentary debates has no direct relevance to the issues the court is called upon to decide in compatibility cases and, hence, these debates are not a proper matter for investigation or consideration by the courts. In particular, it is a cardinal constitutional principle that the will of Parliament is expressed in the language used by it in its enactments. The proportionality of legislation is to be judged on that basis. The courts are to have due regard to the legislation as an expression of the will of Parliament. The proportionality of a statutory measure is not to be judged by the quality of the reasons advanced in support of it in the course of parliamentary debate, or by the subjective state of mind of individual ministers or other members.'

Multiple Choice Questions

Question 1

You are representing a client who is being prosecuted under the (fictitious) Dangerous Breeds of Dog Act 1999 after his 'XL Bully' dog was out of control and bit three people. It is not clear whether the type of dog – 'XL Bully' – is a dog that is bred for fighting and no order has been made by the secretary of state under section 1(c) with regards to this particular type of dog.

In coming to its decision, the court makes a statement explaining the rational for their verdict:

'The statute must be interpreted in light of the law of the land, and Parliament have, in creating this law, made clear which dogs are to apply to the law of land as being a dangerous dog.'

Which rule of interpretation has the court used here?

A. The literal rule.
B. The golden rule.
C. The purposive rule.
D. The mischief rule.
E. The absurd rule.

Question 2

You are defending a civil matter whereby your client, the defendant, is the employer of the claimant, who was injured in an ambulance by a faulty bed. You are arguing that the matter should have proceeded by way of a road traffic accident, and the claimant is arguing that the injury and circumstances were in the course of the claimant's employment, and accordingly should be classed as an employer's liability matter. The distinction is extremely important when the matter of legal costs is to be decided.

The court has referred to the provisions of the Road Traffic Act 1988 in order to come to their decision.

By making reference to the Road Traffic Act 1988 the courts have utilised:

A. It is an extrinsic aid.
B. It is an internal aid.
C. It is the purposive rule.
D. It is an example of ejusdem generis.
E. It is an example of noscitur a sociis.

Question 3

The (fictional) Clear Air Act was enacted to assist with ensuring that the air outside is cleaner and focusses on the use of low emission vehicles, to ensure air quality at all times. Your client, who owns a garage of exotic vehicles, is seeking advice on the Act and how it would apply to his motorcycles and his rickshaws. You have researched the Act in depth and have noted that a peer in the House of Lords has made a detailed statement indicating that it is now a priority of the government to ensure air quality increases by lowering toxic NO2 gas emissions. Further research indicates that a vehicle also includes motorcycles. Rickshaws have three wheels and use more petrol than motorcycles but are not mentioned. The preamble of the Act also provides the rationale for the legislation.

On the question of the rickshaw, which of the following guidelines for interpreting the Act is most likely to be applicable?

A. Purposive approach.
B. The golden rule.
C. The mischief rule.
D. The literal rule.
E. The rule in *Pepper v Hart*.

PART

4

The Courts and Their Role in the Doctrine of Judicial Precedent

4 Judicial Structures Within the Courts

4.1 SQE1 Syllabus

The judiciary and court hierarchy.

4.2 Chapter Overview

This chapter will provide an overview of the current judicial structures in England and Wales. It begins with a broad overview of the judiciary and court systems, before focussing on judges and other legal personnel in the civil courts and the criminal courts. The chapter will also provide an overview on juries in the criminal courts and further court personnel, such as tribunal judges, arbitrators and mediators.

4.3 An Overview of Judiciary and the Court System

The structure of the judiciary can be found within a number of areas such as: the judicial Executive board, the tribunals judicial Executive board, the judges' council and the judicial office.

The enactment of the Constitutional Reform Act 2005 created the office of the Lord Chief Justice as the Head of Judiciary and president of the courts of England and Wales, and restructured the office of Lord Chancellor, to ensure a better fit with the separation of powers. The judiciary is completed via the Judicial Executive Board and the Judges' Council.

Further, enactment of the Tribunals, Courts and Enforcements Act 2007, in addition to unifying the tribunal structures within England and Wales, also created the office of Senior President of Tribunals. The current Senior President of Tribunals completes responsibilities for the tribunal judicial Executive board.

The judicial office now has over 200 staff, and also includes support for judges, in addition also encompassing bodies such as The Judicial College, Human Resources Department, Communications Office and the conduct investigations office.

DOI: 10.4324/9781003435525-9

4.3.1 Overview of the Court System of England and Wales

Whilst we will see the importance of the current court system and structure in the next chapter in relation to judicial precedent, it is important to note that the structure of the courts (Figure 4.1) is based around a higher and lower court system, whereby the decisions of higher courts will be followed by those in the lower courts.

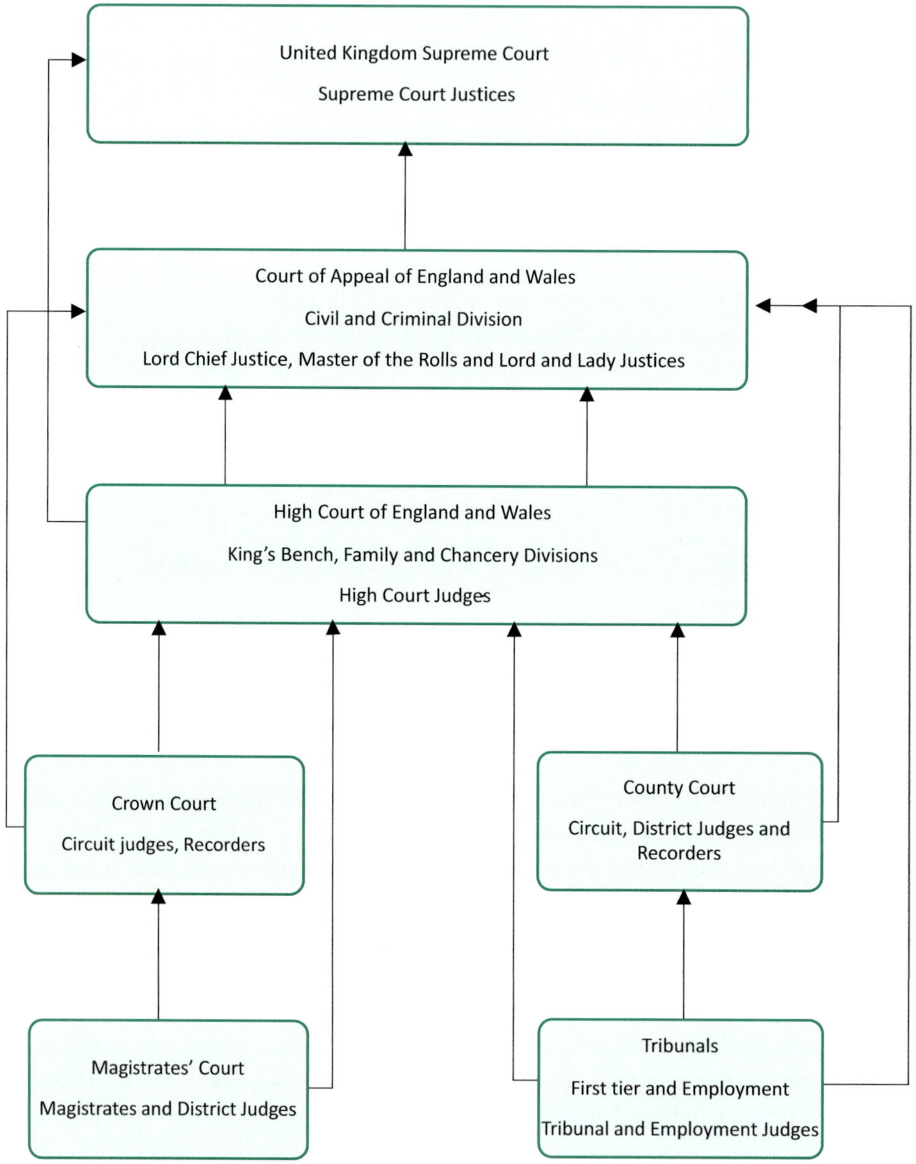

Figure 4.1 Overview of the court system of England and Wales

The arrows signify which courts that a lower court refers to. Furthermore, and in reverse, the higher up the system you proceed, the more weight in terms of legal precedent, is added to any decision, which inferior courts are then expected to utilise as part of their decision-making process.

4.3.2 Supreme Court

The UK Supreme Court was established by the Constitutional Reform Act 2005 and replaced the House of Lords. Based at Middlesex Guild Hall, it now depicts a visual and applicable separation of powers in the United Kingdom Constitution. The Court represents the final appeal court, where cases of the utmost importance in terms of law and public policy are decided.

4.3.3 Senior Courts of England and Wales

Below the Supreme Court is what is known as the Senior Courts of England and Wales, which includes the Court of Appeal and the High Court of Justice. The Court of Appeal is an appellate court, split into Civil and Criminal Divisions and will listen to appeals that are made from the lower courts. The court came into being with the Judicature Acts 1873–1875 and the Appellate Jurisdiction Act 1876. The High Court was also established by the Judicature Acts and amalgamated the existing court system under one unified court. There are currently three divisions of the High Court – the Chancery Division, the Family Division and the King's Bench Division. These divisions will listen to more serious and higher value civil law and family law matters at first instance, but also have the authority to listen to appeals from the lower courts.

4.3.4 Lower Courts

Finally, the lower courts encompass the county court and the Family Court, who listen to civil and family matters respectively, alongside the criminal side of the Magistrates' Court and the Crown Court who listen to summary offences and indictable offences respectively. It is important to note that all criminal matters commence in the Magistrates', before being moved to the Crown Court if the offence is one of a serious nature (indictable offence), or the defendant elects a trial by jury if the offence is deemed to be an 'either-way' offence.

4.3.5 Tribunals

Running parallel to the courts structure, is an intricate system of tribunals. Introduced by the Tribunals, Courts and Enforcement Act 2007 and overseen by the Senior President of Tribunals, there are a number of tribunals that are utilised to manage a number of disputes, such as those in employment and immigration asylum. Tribunals are split into First-tier and Upper Tribunal, and Employment Tribunal and Employment Appeal Tribunal. Appeals to the Court of Appeal can be made from these tribunals (Employment Appeal and Upper Tribunal).

4.4 The Civil Courts

Civil justice encompasses a wide range of matters in which individuals, businesses or organizations seek to resolve disputes or protect their rights. This jurisdiction covers a wide spectrum ranging from minor claims, such as damaged goods or debt recovery, to major disputes between multinational corporations. In many cases, civil disputes are resolved outside of court through established complaints procedures, negotiation or mediation. However, for those cases that do proceed to court, the majority are heard in the county court in England and Wales, while more substantial or complex cases may begin in the High Court.

In civil matters, most cases are conducted in open court, allowing the public to attend.

Judges in these cases typically award financial damages to the successful party, the amount of which depends on the circumstances of the claim. In some instances, the court may issue an order or injunction to enforce certain behaviour or prevent certain actions. Equitable remedies like specific performance can also be ordered. Additionally, the civil courts have mechanisms in place to ensure that awarded damages can be enforced.

4.4.1 County Court Personnel

Approximately 80% of civil and family law work is conducted in the county courts, and as such, a number of judges and other personnel will have an impact upon any matter, judicially or administratively.

District Judges

District Judges sit predominantly in civil and family law matters, and provide judicial decision making on a wide range of matters including actions for damages and injunctions; property disputes involving landlords, tenants, mortgage borrowers and associated possession proceedings; family law matters including divorce and associated matters, such as finance, children and assets, injunctions for domestic violence and antisocial behaviour; court of protection; committal hearings (for example those under CPR Part 81); and insolvency proceedings.

By contrast, Deputy District Judges share the same jurisdiction and power as that of District Judges and generally sit for between 15 and 50 days a year on a fee paid basis in the county courts and district registries of the High Court.

The Judicial Appointments Commission is responsible for administering the recruitment process for District Judges, who, following the process, are formally appointed by the King. Pre-requisites require potential District Judges to have prior legal experience such as that of a practising barrister, solicitor or legal Executive.

Circuit Judges

There are approximately 600 Circuit Judges in England and Wales, who undertake judicial roles in a number of areas. There are six circuits in England and Wales, and a circuit judge will sit in one of those circuits. Their roles are multifaceted, and unlike District Judges, circuit judges will sit in either civil or criminal matters, or specialise in an area such as Chancery or one of the other divisional courts. The Lord Chief Justice is also able to invite circuit judges to sit in the Criminal Division of the Court of Appeal.

The Judicial Appointments Commission is responsible for administering the recruitment process for circuit judges, who following the process, are formally appointed by the King. Circuit judges are required to be lawyers who have previously advocated in court, and hold 'right of audience' for a minimum of seven years. Additionally, they could have been appointed and held a position of recorder, High Court Master or District Judge for at least three years.

Recorders and Assistant Recorders

Recorders sit in both civil and criminal courts of first instance and is usually the initial step for those seeking a judicial role. They are required to determine outcomes in contested matters and applications. They will handle less complex matters.

The Judicial Appointments Commission is responsible for administering the recruitment process for Recorders, who following the process, are formally appointed by the King.

A recorder will sit for approximately 30 days per year, will sit with a circuit judge for one week and will also be supervised in their first week of sitting as a recorder.

Administrative Staff

These are staff that are Ministry of Justice employed, who assist with the day to day running of the court by completing administrative tasks, such as listing the hearings and issuing claim forms.

Court Managers

With a sole administrative role, the Court Manager has operational control over the administrative element of the court including its processes.

Ushers and Clerks

Ushers have the role of directing where parties sit in the hearing and ensuring that oaths and affirmations are taken from witnesses.

Clerks, on the other hand, are sat in front of the judge, and will assist the judges with the case at hand. Their role is to ensure the case progresses with fluidity, and will also keep records of the hearing, and those attending. It is important to note that clerks are not always present in the civil courts.

4.4.2 High Court Personnel

Judges based in the High Court are known, quite simply as High Court Judges. The High Court deals with more complex matters usually in terms of value. High Court Judges will sit in the King's Bench Division, The Family Division or the Chancery Division.

The Judicial Appointments Commission is responsible for administering the recruitment process for High Court Judges, who following the process, are formally appointed by the King.

4.5 The Criminal Courts

Once the Crown Prosecution Service has made the decision to prosecute a suspect, criminal matters are brought before a court in order to administer justice. In the Magistrates' court, a panel of three Magistrates or a District Judge hears more than 95% of the cases. They consider the facts and weigh the evidence prior to concluding whether the suspect is guilty or innocent. If the offender is found guilty, the Magistrates or District Judge (in the Magistrates' Court) will determine the sentence and may also send the case to the Crown Court for sentencing.

The more serious criminal cases are heard in the Crown Court, where they are often tried by a circuit judge, recorder or, in the worst cases, a High Court Judge sitting with a jury.

4.5.1 Magistrates' Court Personnel

Magistrates

Magistrates are one of the most unique and traditional cornerstones of the English and Welsh Legal System. They are undertaking a voluntary role and administer justice in summary criminal matters. They are unqualified, but trained, and are members of the local community. Magistrates sit tripartite, with the court legal advisor, but can also sit in a pair. Magistrates have the authority to sentence defendants that are guilty.

Legal Advisor/Court Associate

The court legal advisor is there due to the Magistrates being unqualified, and is a trained and qualified legal personnel, such as a solicitor or barrister. They advise the Magistrates as to the law on matters before them.

The court associate, by comparison, is similar to that of the clerk in the civil courts. They ensure accuracy with regards to the trial.

District Judge

A District Judge can also oversee proceedings in the Magistrates' courts, and will sit on their own, usually on more serious matters.

Usher

The Usher, like that of the civil court, has a duty to ensure that correct places are assigned to all parties that are present at trial, and the room is adequately prepared.

4.5.2 Crown Court Personnel

Criminal matters that are tried in the Crown Court are usually heard by Circuit Judges (discussed at 4.4.1). Matters of a less complex nature are sometimes heard by recorders.

Other personnel present at Crown Trials will be those mentioned earlier, such as court clerks, who ensure evidence is presented and available to assist the Judges and will also assist with oaths and affirmations from the witnesses and jury members.

4.5.3 Juries in the Crown Court

Historically speaking, trial by jury has been a significant cornerstone of the English legal system. The idea that a defendant/suspect is tried by 12 members of the public leads to a criminal process that is wholly fair and just. It promotes the freedom of fair trials and that every defendant has the right to a trial by jury on the basis of the charges and a not guilty plea.

Juries listen intently to the case at hand – they can decide in their deliberations prior to a verdict whether the prosecution has proved their case, and their decisions are based on the evidence that is put before them in court.

As part of their deliberations, they must choose to either convict and find the defendant guilty, or acquit, and not guilty of the charge (of course, jurors in cases of multiple charges can find the defendant guilty of some charges, and not guilty for others).

The burden of proof is one that must be beyond all reasonable doubt, and unanimous verdicts are required. A majority verdict in some cases may be accepted. This could be the case where the jury has failed to reach a unanimous verdict after spending a reasonable amount of time deliberating. It is important to note that in the event a guilty verdict is declared, the judge overseeing the case – usually a circuit judge or recorder – will then pass down an appropriate sentence which will be derived from the sentencing guidelines.

If a verdict cannot be reached in the majority, then a jury will be 'hung,' meaning in the event the Crown wished to prosecute, they will be required to do so with a new jury in place.

Jurors are selected at random from the electoral roll.

4.6 Further Court Personnel

In addition to the court personnel mentioned, there are also further personnel who will play a role in judicial proceedings either prior to the issue of court proceedings, during and after the matter at hand has been concluded.

4.6.1 Senior Judiciary

Court of Appeal

It would be prudent to start with senior judiciary, and in particular Court of Appeal judges. The appeal courts are senior courts in the English and Welsh Legal System. The Court of Appeal is split into the Criminal Division and the Civil Division.

Here, you will find, the Lord and Lady Chief Justice, along with the Master of the Rolls. It also consists of the 'ordinary' Lord and Lady Justices of Appeal and the Heads of Division of the High Court.

The Criminal Division of the Court of Appeal is led by the Lord/Lady Chief Justice and will hear appeals from the Crown Court.

The Civil Division, by contrast, is led by the Master of the Rolls and will hear appeals from the High Court and county courts, as well as tribunals.

The Judicial Appointments Commission is responsible for administering the recruitment process for Court of Appeal judges via a selection panel, who following the process, are formally appointed by the King. Pre-requisites require potential judges to be senior with substantial judicial experience.

Supreme Court

The Supreme Court is the court of last instance in the United Kingdom and hears cases that are appealed from the lower courts, including the Court of Appeal (both civil and criminal), the High Court in some exceptional circumstances, the Court of Session and the Court of Appeal in Northern Ireland, and its High Court in some exceptional circumstances.

The appointment of Supreme Court judges can be found in section 25 of the Constitutional Reform Act 2005, and general prerequisites are to have held high judicial office for at least two years. Section 60 of the Constitutional Reform Act 2005 describes that as having sat in the Court of Appeal or High Court (England, Wales and Northern Ireland), or the Court of Session (Scotland).

Another route would be that of qualifying practitioner – here, an experienced barrister or solicitor with a minimum of 15 years of experience. The same would apply for advocates in Scotland, and solicitors who are able to appear in the Court of Session, or members of the Bar of Northern Ireland, or solicitors.

An independent selection commission oversees the process for appointment of UKSC judges. This process is governed by sections 26 to 27b of the Constitutional Reform Act 2005 and the Supreme Court (Judicial Appointments) Regulations 2013.

4.6.2 Tribunal Personnel, Arbitrators and Mediators

Tribunal Personnel

Judges who sit in tribunals are a part of a specialist body that deals with specific areas of law, such as disputes in the workplace and decisions made by government departments that affect individuals in matters concerning immigration status and asylum, the welfare system and tax credits.

The Tribunals, Courts and Enforcement Act 2007 was enacted to unify the UK tribunal system by introducing a two-tiered approach, allowing for more clarity and transparency in the tribunal system.

Furthermore, section 1 of the Act allows for tribunal personnel, who are legally qualified, to be given the same status as the judiciary, with a guarantee of judicial independence.

The majority of tribunal hearings are heard by tribunal judges who are legally qualified and appointed by virtue of schedule 2 (1) and (2) and schedule 3 (1) and (2) of the Tribunals, Courts and Enforcement Act 2007. In addition, tribunal judges will sometimes sit with tribunal members, who are often non-legal experts, with particular expertise in relation to the matter at hand. Their role is to provide an alternative viewpoint to proceedings and will also sometimes question the parties and witness when relevant. Given their non-legal background, they will be advised on any points of law by tribunal judges.

Arbitrators

Arbitration in England and Wales is governed by the Arbitration Act 1996. In the context of commercial dispute resolution, arbitration clauses/agreements are popular given their propensity to resolve disputes privately, quickly and without being led by the court's processes in terms of time and cost. As such, an arbitrator is usually a legally qualified professional who will listen to the matter at hand at a hearing and make a decision that will be binding upon the parties. The flexibility of arbitration means that parties can jointly agree upon a preferred arbitrator and allows for commercial relationships to continue given its tendency to be more flexible than litigation. If an arbitration agreement exists, and litigation has been commenced, then by virtue of section 9, a stay of legal proceedings can be sought to ensure that jurisdiction of the matter is with the arbitrator. However, section 9(3) provides that such a stay in proceedings will not be granted in the event proceedings have been advanced by both parties.

Mediators

Following the Woolf and Jackson reforms, mediation now forms a key part of the litigation process, with adverse costs penalties being awarded against those parties who fail to participate in mediation when the opportunity arises. The Civil Procedural Rules encourages the use of alternative methods of dispute resolution and by virtue of P1.4(I), the Court must further the overriding objective by actively managing cases; P26.4(1), A party may, when filing the completed Allocation Questionnaire, make a request for proceedings to be stayed to try and settle the case by ADR and P26.4(2)(b). The court may stay proceedings on its own initiative, if it considers that such a stay would be appropriate. Accordingly, the failure to advise on alternative methods of dispute resolution may constitute negligence, and breach of principle 4 of the SRA's code of conduct – failing to act in the best interests of the client.

A mediator will work with both parties in individual caucus sessions in an attempt to narrow the issues. They do not decide matters in the same way as judges and allow the parties to resolve their disputes on their own terms by assisting them in reaching an agreement.

In the event a settlement does not materialise, then the litigation can commence (or resume if stayed).

Chapter 4 Revision Points

This chapter has provided you with an overview of the court structure and the types of judges that are present in those courts.

It is important to check your knowledge using the following Multiple Choice Questions.

Multiple Choice Questions

Question 1

In which court is it possible for a non-legally qualified person who has non law expertise in another area be able to work within the judicial system as a judge?

A. Employment Tribunal but not the Crown Court.
B. The Divisional Courts but not the county court.
C. The Family Courts but not the Magistrates' Court.
D. The Magistrates' Court without a legal advisor, but not an Employment Tribunal.
E. The Crown Court but not the High Court.

Question 2

You are acting on behalf of a client who has been charged with an indictable offence, which is set for a trial in the Old Bailey.

When deciding on whether your client is guilty or not guilty, who of the following will decide such guilt?

A. A Magistrate, but not a jury.
B. A jury, but not a Circuit Judge.
C. A jury and a Circuit Judge.
D. A District Judge and a legal advisor.
E. A jury and a District Judge.

Question 3

A District Judge is hearing a complex landlord and tenant matter. Both parties are represented by barristers, however, it is clear to the judge that the parties are not being truthful in the presentation of their evidence.

What could the judge do when making her decision?

A. She should listen to the evidence carefully and make a decision that is based solely on the facts and evidence as submitted by the parties.
B. The judge should be very careful proceeding, as the wrong decision could lead to a disciplinary action against her.
C. She should make a decision, and if an appeal is made based upon an error, the parties can apply to the Family Division of the High Court.
D. She could seek assistance from the court's legal advisor.
E. She can adjourn the case and ask a more experienced judge to make a decision.

5 Sources of Law – The Courts and Precedent

5.1 SQE1 Syllabus

Development of case law: The doctrine of precedent, court hierarchy.

5.2 Chapter Overview

This chapter will provide an overview of the common law, and how the doctrine of judicial precedent operates in the Legal System of England and Wales. The chapter will also focus on how precedent operates within court hierarchical structures and tribunals.

5.3 Introduction to the Common Law

We briefly touched upon the concept of common law in Chapter 1, and this section will allow us to delve deeper into the concept. Simply put, common law is judge made law, or rather, decisions reached by judges in cases that create legal principles that inform future similar cases, by providing clarity and consistency. It is also sometimes referred to as case law.

The common law is not a new phenomenon and can trace its roots back almost 900 years, where the court system in England and Wales was made into a more unified system of justice which eventually would be named the common law. As the system began to crystallise, the 'common' law of the land would be applicable in all his (and her) Majesty's courts, moving away from early Norman justice methods, where local community law was encouraged but did involve inconsistent decisions.

As mentioned, the common law is judge-made law, which is based around their decisions in cases. In the Crown's adversarial system of justice, these laws were based upon the submission of legal points by both party's legal representatives. To ensure credibility and consistency in the system, the system of judicial precedent was also instituted, which allows for a very detailed system of judicial reasoning, which judges would go great lengths to do. When you, in your capacity as a solicitor, read a judgment that is more than 100 pages long, part of that, is the notion

DOI: 10.4324/9781003435525-10

that a judge wants to very clearly justify why a decision is being reached. That is extremely important, as that decision will then set a legal precedent, which will be followed by the courts in any cases that are similar in the future that compare factually and legally. Legal precedent is created in accordance with the Latin maxim, '*stare decisis*.' Although the common law is designed to be rigid due its advantage of creating consistency, it also has the ability to be flexible as judges can derogate from previous legal precedents in very specific circumstances, especially if a previous precedent could cause a result that is unfair.

5.3.1 Criticisms?

The main criticism that will attach to the common law is the notion that judges are creating the law. Judicial activism, as it is otherwise called, is a criticism against non-elected judges deciding cases (and thus making the law) in a democratic state whereby Parliament is the supreme law-making body, who are, in the House of Commons at least, elected. However, it would be fair to state that Parliament could not possibly legislate on everything, and the concept of judge made law, which follows a clear precedent in a court hierarchy, brings consistency and clarity. And secondly, whilst the common law is judge made, judges cannot declare Acts of Parliament as invalid, and cannot question the validity of an Act or its creation as per the doctrine of Parliamentary Sovereignty. Judges will give effect to the will of Parliament and the purpose of the Act when deciding cases involving primary legislation, by interpreting the statutes, as we already know.

5.3.2 Parliamentary Sovereignty and the Common Law

Given the doctrine of Parliamentary Sovereignty, primary legislation enacted will overrule any common law legal principles. An advantage of this feat is that Parliament can use legislation to quickly change any common law precedents that may now be problematic, due to changes in, for example, the society and the economy. Going back to our examples of contract law, this is an area of law which has been developed mainly via the common law with use of judge made precedents. However, from time to time, legislation has been enacted to assist the area to ensure that legal precedent is superseded by legislation and updated.

5.3.3 Example

For example, section 2(1) of the Unfair Contract Terms Act 1977 brought in the rule that exclusion clauses could no longer exclude liability for death and personal injury for negligence, something which contractually, parties were able to contract out of.

Another example is the Misrepresentation Act 1967, which updated the vitiating factor of misrepresentation in the law of contract. Initially, this involved two categories of either 'fraudulent' and 'innocent' misrepresentation (whereby the very strict threshold for proving fraudulent misrepresentation often led to many falling into the 'innocent' category) to introducing an additional 'statutory tort' which allowed innocent parties to claim damages where negligent (and some innocent) misrepresentation had been made. Section 2 now is the most important source of right to claim damages for misrepresentation. The Act itself also removed certain bars to recission in section 1. Thus, clearly, the common law and statutory law can work in tandem. In addition, judges can, as part of their decision-making process, recommend law reform in obiter dicta (said 'by the way'), particularly in older statutes, or even deem laws to be incompatible with human rights principles, which does not question the validity of an Act of Parliament, but does notify Parliament that statutory law may not be compatible with the European Convention on Human Rights.

The common law is a feature of many legal systems in the world, but its origin is England. Its credibility in creating consistency and clarity is the reason why it still exists in many jurisdictions across the globe, including the USA, Canada and Australia. The other popular system is a civil law system, based around the influences of Roman Law, Continental Law and Napoleonic Law. These systems are based upon codes that are primary sources of law. These codes may include the law of persons, commercial law and obligations. Decisions of judges are based upon the codes enshrined in their legal systems as opposed to legal precedents.

5.4 The Doctrine of Judicial Precedent

As mentioned earlier in 3.3, the doctrine of judicial precedent (or precedent) is the key that has enabled the common law to grow and develop. Its mere development has led to clear consistency in terms of decision making and clarity, so much so, that the law becomes clear in those areas where a clear precedent has been set. These precedents can then be used as legal authority in later comparable cases.

5.5 Precedent in Practice

5.5.1 Ratio Decidendi and Stare Decisis

As mentioned earlier, judges are individuals who listen to cases before them impartially and deliver a judgment based upon what they have heard. The judgment will contain what is commonly referred to as the *ratio decidendi*, which can be loosely translated to the 'reasons for the decision.' You will often come across the term as the 'ratio' of a case. The ratio of a case is what forms the binding precedent which will then be expected to be followed by inferior courts. We look at this in more depth at 5.5.1 and 5.5.3.

When determining the ratio, a judge will focus on the facts (which is how a ratio can be distinguished from obiter dicta), which will have been presented by the parties, and analyse the same. The judge will then apply any pre-existing legal statutes/common law principles to the facts. This then creates the basis of precedent for the future, which is binding firstly on the parties at hand, and the future for judges. The maxim *stare decisis* becomes applicable – 'let the decision stand' (and 'do not unsettle the established') in future cases with very similar material facts that come before judges. The hierarchy of the courts once again comes into play here.

Persuasive Precedent and Obiter Dicta

Persuasive precedent, also known as persuasive authority, is non-binding. Persuasive precedent may be of interest to the judge, or the judge could refer to something said as a dissenting judgment in a previous case, or a statement made by obiter by another judge. Persuasive precedent can originate from inferior courts, as well as courts of even authority. In areas of little to no legal precedent, judgment from foreign courts could be used as persuasive precedent in order to provide context for a specific legal point. This often is the case when a decision of the Privy Council is cited. For example, in the case of *Caldwell v Maguire & Fitzgerald* [2001] EWCA Civ 1054, the learned judge referred to the Australian case of *Rootes v Shelton* [1968] ALR 33 to determine the standard of the duty of care owed in sporting contests, and the acceptance of inherent risks of such sporting contests.

Obiter Dicta (sometimes referred to as 'obiter' or 'dicta') can be loosely translated to 'things said by the way.' This, again, can be used persuasively in future cases. In any ratio, the key element is the decision. Any statements made by a judge that lead to the decision are not binding. An obiter statement may be very brief, or even contain a hypothetical example to provide more context for the resulting ratio.

It is important to note that an obiter statement and persuasive precedent are non-binding.

5.5.2 Precedent Case Example

Let's have a look at the case of *R v R* [1991] UKHL 12, [1991] 3 WLR 767.

This case involved the conviction of a male who pled guilty of attempted rape and assault occasioning actual bodily harm. The victim in this matter was his wife. The wife had left the matrimonial home, but divorce proceedings had not been instituted before the offence.

The defendant, after his conviction of attempted rape, appealed to the Court of Appeal on the grounds that the judge at first instance had erred in the application of the law as a man may rape his wife due to the consent that is given in entering the contract of marriage, of which had not been revoked – either by a court or the parties.

The Court of Appeal dismissed his appeal but delivered a reserved judgment due to the 'question of general public importance set out' and granted leave to appeal to the House of Lords.

At the House of Lords, the basis of the defendant's submissions revolved around a proposition made by Sir Matthew Hale in 1736,[1] that a husband could not be guilty of raping his lawful wife, due to the matrimonial contract (and thus consent) between them, to which she could not retract. There were further mentions of this 'common law rule' in Treatise of the Pleas of the Crown in 1803 and Archbold, Pleading and Evidence in Criminal Cases in 1822. There was no further mention of this so-called common law exemption for marital rape in the almost two centuries in the lead up to the case at hand·

Lord Kieth, delivering the leading judgment, analysed cases that had been decided previously based upon marital rape. He also analysed the common law rule that Sir Matthew Hale had mentioned in 1736. He then provided an interpretation of the term 'unlawful' under section 1 of the Sexual Offences (Amendment) Act 1976 and was satisfied that 'unlawful' in the Act was not 'outside the bonds of marriage,' but doing something which is contrary to the law without justification or excuse.

He then finished by applying the law to the matter, which then created the ratio and the precedent.

> The remaining and no less difficult question is whether, despite that view, this is an area where the court should step aside to leave the matter to the Parliamentary process. *This is not the creation of a new offence; it is the removal of a common law fiction which has become anachronistic and offensive, and we consider that it is our duty having reached that conclusion to act upon it* (emphasis added).

Thus, a proposition in common law which was outdated and abhorrent resulted in a new precedent being set, which would have become binding on every court given the House of Lord's superiority, as being the highest court in the land. The precedent and Lord Kieth in this case also provided an excellent overview of the common law and its advantages:

> an example of the common law evolving in the light of changing social, economic and cultural developments.
>
> Lord Kieth of Kinkel, *R v R* [1991] UKHL 12, [1991] 3 WLR 767

1 *History of the Pleas of the Crown* (1st edition 1736), vol. 1, ch. 58, p. 629.

The example that we have used is one that shows the flexibility of the common law whereby cases can be overruled in the face of changing attitudes in society. Lord Kieth did refer to examples in his judgment of cases the appellant did raise in support of his appeal – namely decided cases that did acknowledge (and sometimes support) the exception as proposed by Sir Matthew Hale. These cases were *R v Clarence* (1888) 22 QBD 23, *R v Clarle* [1949] 2 All ER 448, *R v Miller* [1954] 2 QB 282, *R v Reid* [1973] QB 299, *R v O'Brien (Edward)* [1974] 3 All ER 663 and *R v Steele* (1976) 65 CR App R. 22.

5.5.3 Precedent Advantages and Disadvantages

There are some very clear advantages of using judicial precedent. Some of these are the doctrine promotes certainty, uniformity, flexibility and a clear structure for inferior courts to follow in terms of decision making. This promotes legal certainty and ensures that there is a clear access to justice and decisions are made in accordance with the rule of law.

There are also some clear disadvantages, some of which have been highlighted in 5.3.1. These revolve around judges making the law, but also bad precedents being very difficult to overturn unless statutory changes are made, or the precedent is overruled at an appropriate court.

5.5.4 Precedent and Hierarchy

In order to ensure that the system of precedent would work effectively, a hierarchical structure of the courts had to be created that would revolved around the concept that lower courts would be bound by the judgments of the higher courts. The Judicature Acts of 1873–1875 created a restructure of the courts (the first of its kind since English law began), which was further crystallised when the House of Lords (now Supreme Court) became the court of last instance (or final appeal) after the enactment of the Appellate Jurisdiction Act 1876. Furthermore, the Acts also revolutionised the way the rules and remedies of equity were dispensed, with equity courts and common law courts being able to apply each within their respective courts.

Let's retake a look at the court hierarchy:

Figure 5.1 shows a clear structure as to which courts can appeal to whom. The same also gives you an idea of how the hierarchy of courts would work in the sense of judges in the lower courts following the decisions of judges in the higher courts. As such, judges in the lower courts will be bound by the decisions of the judges in the High Court, Court of Appeal and the Supreme Court. Court of Appeal decisions will bind the High Court, but not the Supreme Court. It is important to note that precedent also binds some courts where the decision has been made. For example, the Civil Division of the Court of Appeal is bound by its own previous decisions with three exceptions to that rule. Firstly, the court can derogate from a previous binding decision where it conflicts with a later decision of the Supreme Court; secondly, where there are two previous conflicting decisions, the Court of

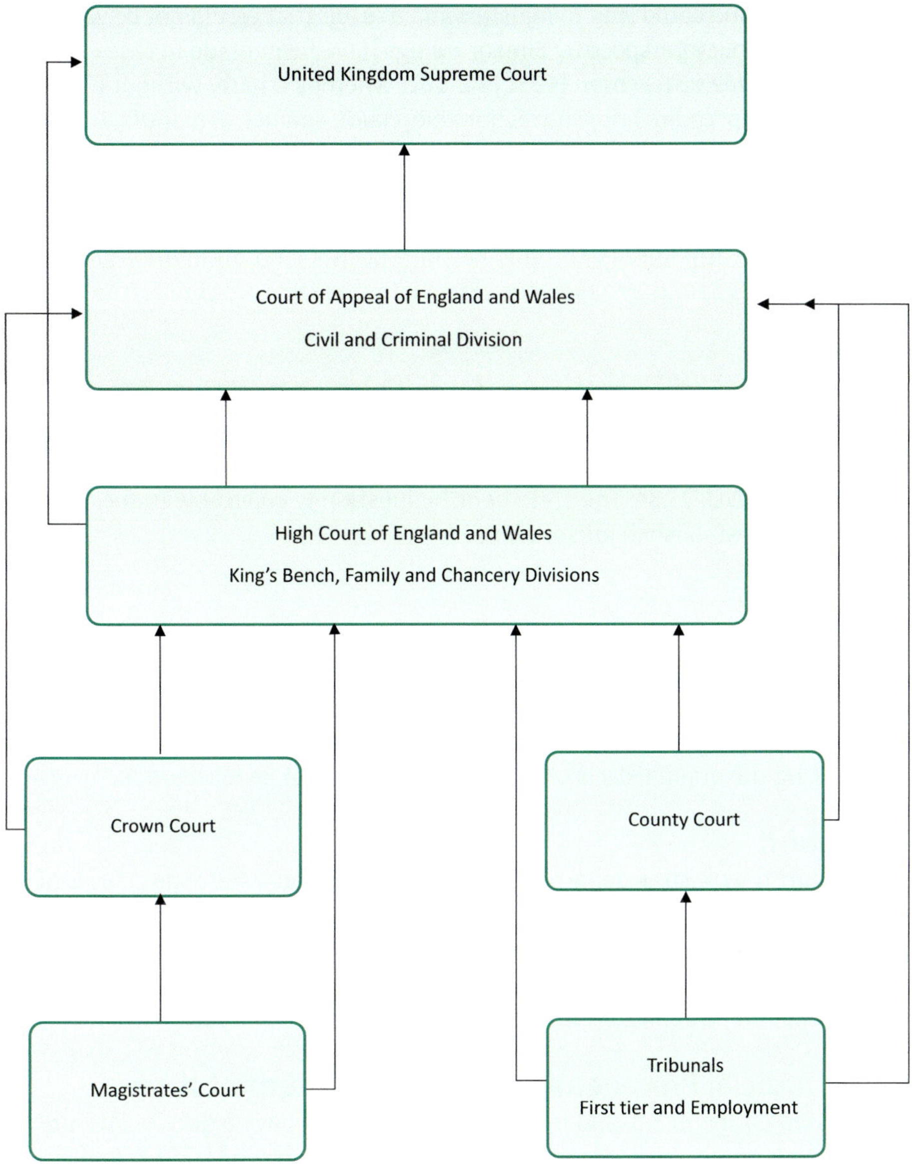

Figure 5.1 The court hierarchy

Appeal must therefore make a decision on the conflict in a present third case; and finally, where a previous decision was made *per incuriam*. These will be discussed in more depth in 5.5.6.

Precedent Application Tools

As discussed earlier, it is important to note that the maxim of stare decisis is that a court should stand by a decided matter in any judgment and should follow precedent. However, as we saw from our example in *R v R*, this is not always the best outcome, and could lead to injustice and a result that would not be welcomed from a public policy perspective. Similar rulings have been made in case examples such as *Donoghue v Stevenson* [1932] AC 562, whereby a party without a contractual relationship could bring an actionable claim against a manufacturer of a product.

Follow the Case

This rule stringently follows the rule of stare decisis, and an inferior or court of even authority is bound by a previous case where the facts are similar/the same.

Overrule

This, in simple terms, is when a court decided to overrule legal principles set by an inferior court, which means the law is no longer correct. The Supreme Court can depart from a previously decided case following the issue of the Practice Statement [1966] 1 WLR 1234. The statement in question is applicable to the Supreme Court given its established jurisprudence.[2]

Reverse

Sometimes, the decisions of the lower courts are appealed to the higher courts. In such an instance, the higher court will either agree with the decision of the court of first instance, and thus the law being correct. The appeal courts can also disagree with the judge at first instance, and such a case would reverse the decision, thus, making the original decision as one that should not be relied upon.

Distinguish

Here, a court may wish to depart from a previous decision, where the court is of the opinion that there are differences between the present case, and the case in which the precedent had been set. To this end, the court is not overruling, or deeming the law to be incorrect, rather it has decided that the application of that particular precedent would not be applicable due to the differences in the factual matrix.

5.5.5 Judicial Precedent and Statutory Interpretation

As discussed earlier in 5.3, and in Chapter 4, the courts have a duty to interpret an Act of Parliament in a manner that gives effect to the interpretation of Parliament, by construing the Act in full.

As we have seen, there is a statutory interpretation framework that also applies, in the event the courts are having to deal with any aspects of an Act that may be ambiguous.

It is crucial to note that Acts of Parliament are the highest form of law in the land and take precedence over the common law. Statutes can be created to replace the common law, especially in areas where the law requires a material change.

2 *Austin v Mayor and Burgesses of the London Borough of Southwark* [2010] UKSC 28.

5.5.6 Precedent, Courts and Tribunals

We know that the hierarchy of courts plays an important role in the success of judicial precedent. Stare decisis requires judgments to be followed.

Supreme Court

The Supreme Court was created after the abolishment of the House of Lords with the enactment of the Constitutional Reform Act 2005. Based in Middlesex Guildhall, it now appears to showcase a clear separation from the Houses of Parliament, where the Appellate Committee of the House of Lords was previously based.

Decisions of the Supreme Court are binding upon all courts below them. Prior to the issue of the Practice Statement [1966] 1 WLR 1234, the House of Lords were bound by their own previous decisions. The Practice Statement allowed more tractability in decision making for the court, which also allows the opportunity for injustice.

The Supreme Court is reluctant to use the Practice Statement, with it being used in situations whereby the precedent or its rationale had become outdated or inoperative, or in instances where the changing social and political circumstances warrant such a change, or if the past decision and precedent would lead to an injustice.[3] For example, the decision in *British Railways Board v Herrington* [1972] AC 877 overruled the decision in *Addy & Sons v Dumbreck* [1929] AC 358. The rationale for the change was based upon the original position that the only common law duty applicable to trespassers from occupiers was the duty not to cause deliberate or reckless injury. The House of Lords departed from the decision due to social policy reasons, and the inability of younger trespassers to recognise danger, and the standard of care applicable to occupiers objectively in terms of avoiding danger. The decision in Herrington resulted in Law Commission proposals which resulted in the enactment of the Occupiers' Liability Act 1984.[4]

It is also important to note that the Supreme Court will be reluctant to depart from any case law where Parliament has approved the rule in question or where the case law related to a construction of a statute. One of the main criticisms of judicial precedent (or judge made law), is the fact that judges are not elected, and by creating precedent and the common law, are in effect law making.

Court of Appeal

The Judicature Act of 1873 and 1875 created for a more streamlined court system, and one of its main introductions was the Court of Appeal.

3 *British Railways Board v Herrington* [1972] AC 877 overruled *Addy & Sons v Dumbreck* [1929] AC 358.

4 Law Commission Report on Liability for Damage or Injury to Trespassers and Related Questions of Occupiers' Liability, LAW COM no 75, March 1976.

The Court of Appeal is only inferior to the Supreme Court and its decisions are binding on all courts that are inferior to them, such as the High Court and courts of first instance.

The Court of Appeal (Civil Division) is bound by its own decisions. However, it can derogate from precedent with the use of three exceptions.[5] The Criminal Division of the Court of Appeal is not bound by its previous decisions, given such decisions revolve around the loss of one's liberty, and if the court of first instance has in some way erred in the application of the law, then this would be corrected. Similarly, if an application is made by the Attorney General or Solicitor General because an 'unduly lenient' sentence may well have been applied by the court at first instance during a sentencing hearing, then this would also be heard. It is easy to see why in such instances, the derogation from previous decisions would be welcome to ensure any injustice in matters involving personal liberty.

The first exception can apply in the event there are two decisions that conflict with one another; the court must then choose one that will set the precedent.

The second exception applies when a previous judgment of the court conflicts with a later Supreme Court judgment. In such an instance, the hierarchy of the courts would mean that the Court of Appeal would not be bound by its older decision, given the later conflicting judgment of the Supreme Court.

The third exception allows the Court of Appeal to not follow its own decision whereby that decision has been delivered *per incuriam*. Simply put, *per incuriam* means a judgment of the court that has been made through a 'lack of care,' in error or ignorance of an existing law that is either statutory or binding precedent.

In the event that an inferior court believes that a decision has been made *per incuriam* the hierarchy of the courts would mean that they must continue to follow that decision as per the *stare decisis* rule.

High Court and Divisional Courts

The High Court, in terms of precedent, for sake of legal certainty, will follow judgments that have been made by other High Court Judges, but they are *not* bound to follow the decisions of the court.[6]

5 *Young v Bristol Aeroplane Ltd* [1944] KB 718 [1944] All ER 293.
6 *Colchester Estates v Carlton Industries* [1986] Ch 80.

The Divisional Court's decisions are binding as it promotes certainty. Further Divisional Court cases are heard by a minimum of two judges. They too, like the Court of Appeal, in the instance of conflicting decisions can choose which precedent to follow.

High Court decisions will bind inferior courts.

Tribunals

From a hierarchical perspective, Employment Appeal Tribunals are bound by the Supreme Court and the Court of Appeal. However, Employment Appeal Tribunals are not required to follow the decisions of the High Court or its own decisions.

Privy Council

The Privy Council are not bound by their own decisions. It is important to note that the Privy Council is a court that deals with matters primarily from the Commonwealth and other UK overseas territories. Thus, the decisions of the courts have no bearing on the hierarchy of the courts. Their decisions could be referred to persuasively.

Court of Justice of the European Union

The decisions of the Court of Justice of the European Union were binding prior to the UK's withdrawal from the European Union. Accordingly, any judgments delivered by the court are no longer applicable to domestic law, unless it falls within the existing rights of those elements that are goverened by the EU Withdrawal Agreement.

Chapter 5 Revision Points

- Common law is a crucial source of law in the English Legal System and has developed over centuries of decision making.
- The Judicature Acts of 1873–1875 and the Appellate Jurisdiction Act 1876 created a more streamlined version of the courts.
- Judicial precedent is a doctrine that is based upon the maxims of *stare decisis* and *ratio decidendi*. These principles dictate judgment to be made in a particular way, clearly citing the reasons for the decision based upon the material facts of the case, and then for such decisions to be followed by inferior courts. The ratio of the case is the binding element.
- Ratios and precedent can be avoided in very specific circumstances through the rules of overruling (higher courts) and distinguishing.
- Some precedent, where not binding, can be used persuasively. Judges may also make statements obiter (things said by the way) as part of their judgments. These statements do not represent the ratio and are not binding.

It is important to check your knowledge using the following Multiple Choice Questions.

Multiple Choice Questions

Question 1

A judge is hearing a matter involving a private Bill where allegations have been made that Parliament was misled in the enactment of such legislation, and thus should not be applicable. There appears to be some accuracy to the allegations that Parliament may have been misled.

When making a decision, what should the judge do?

A. Disapply the Act as reasons for its existence are not accurate as Parliament has been misled.
B. Notwithstanding the alleged misleading of Parliament, a judge's job is to apply the law as it appears in the statute book.
C. The judge can issue a declaration of incompatibility, under the Human Rights Act 1998.
D. As Parliament has been allegedly misled, the judge should distinguish previous case law and set a new precedent to ensure no further injustices can occur.
E. The judge can set a new precedent by making use of the rule of implied repeal and take this opportunity to correct the Act as you see fit.

Question 2

The Civil Division of Court of Appeal is hearing a matter, and it has become evident that there appears to be two conflicting precedents.

Which of the following is the best option for the judges?

A. The judges can utilise the Practice Statement [1966] 1 WLR 1234 in order to choose a decision and set the precedent.
B. The judges in the Court of Appeal are bound by the most recent decisions notwithstanding it conflicts with a previous older decision and must decide the present case the same way.
C. The judges can utilise one of the exceptions available as there are conflicting decisions and choose which one of the precedents to continue with.
D. The judges are not bound by previous decisions and can simply decide the matter as they see fit.
E. The judges can refer the matter to the Supreme Court for a decision because of the conflict.

Question 3

A judge is hearing a complex contract law case in the Chancery Division of the High Court. The case involves privity of contract and the contract in question has been made in favour of a third party, who is now taking legal action in the matter against the parties. There is a very clear precedent (set at the same level), which will favour the defendant, but the judge is aware of a Bill that is due to be granted Royal Assent, which will change the precedent in favour of the claimant.

Which of the following is correct?

A. High Court Judges are bound by previous precedent, and so this must be followed in this matter, as the court binds itself.
B. High Court Judges are not required to follow the precedent and can change, as the court does not bind itself.
C. The precedent is now irrelevant as the Supremacy of Parliament means that the High Court Judge must now give effect to the new Act, as it will apply retrospectively anyway.
D. The High Court Judge is under an obligation to adjourn the matter until the new legislation comes into force, so the correct decision can be applied.
E. The High Court Judge can make a reference to the Court of Appeal to provide clarity on the matter.

PART 5
Hierarchy, Appeals and Jurisdiction

6 Civil Courts

6.1 SQE1 Syllabus

Within the SQE1 syllabus, it is an expectation that knowledge will be demonstrated of the courts, the judiciary, court hierarchy, the appeal system, jurisdiction, rights of audience and the development of case law via the doctrine of precedent.

6.2 Chapter Overview

This chapter ensures that learners have an in-depth understanding of the role that is played by the Civil Courts. It will begin with the role of the county court and will continue to consider the development of cases through the court hierarchy. We will consider the concepts of rights of audience and the role of tribunals and the senior courts.

6.3 The Role of the County Court

Historically, the county courts of England and Wales were established as a means to improve access to justice. Previously, the universal jurisdiction of the High Court ensured that claimants would face an unwieldy and costly journey to have their case heard. This changed with the County Courts Act 1867. Under section 28 of the Act the new county court system was given exclusive jurisdiction over other courts for prescribed purposes.

Today, county courts are usually located within vast combined court centres in which both civil and criminal matters are dealt with alongside family cases and Employment Tribunals. These are located in locations such as Hull, Coventry, Derby, Leeds, Sheffield and Stafford.

It is important to note that these centres are not defined geographically according to the county structure of England and Wales. Instead, they are titled as being located in towns and cities. The reason behind this is again historical with the courts of today evolving from the previous courts that corresponded with county territories.

DOI: 10.4324/9781003435525-12

The county courts traditionally deal with matters that are of lower value in nature. Within the Civil Procedure Rules (CPR), a 'playbook' that manages the conduct of Civil Claims, it is stated that:

> Proceedings (whether for damages or for a specified sum) may only be started in the High Court if the value of the claim is more than £100,000.
>
> CPR Practice Direction (PD) 7A, Para 2.1

It is therefore noted that matters below the £100,000 value will commence in the county court. Attention should also be paid to the word 'may' in the preceding statement. Claimants can commence claims valued at over £100,000 in either the county court or the High Court.

CPR PD 7A also confirms at paragraph 2.2 that:

> Proceedings which include a claim for damages in respect of personal injuries may only be started in the High Court if the value of the claim is £50,000 or more.

Again, matters below £50,000 will tend to be the sole domain of the county court with higher value matters again being such that they can commence in either the county or High Courts.

The county court has jurisdiction in three distinct areas of civil dispute, namely purely civil claims, those involving family disputes and also those in the area of insolvency.

County courts tend to be highly active legal arenas with multiple cases listed within each of the court rooms on any given day. Some of these matters will involve very short inputs with debt and money claims often being the simplest matters of court business. On the other hand, contested contract cases, matters involving the ongoing welfare of children, probate disputes and medical negligence matters may involve many days of court time.

The duration of cases in the county courts are managed via the allocation of claims to one of three tracks. Part 26 of the CPR provides for the allocation of defended cases based upon the value of the sum claimed. The Small Claims Track is used for matters of not more than £10,000. The Fast Track is utilised for claims valued between £10,000 and £25,000, and claims above this upper threshold are allocated to the Multi-Track. The tracks reflect the complexity of the case and correspond to the likely costs, time and resources that will be required to resolve the matter.

6.4 Appeals From the County Court

Whether a case within the county court is in relation to a family matter, employment, commercial or debt, it is typically the case that the final decision can be subject to an appeal. This is where the losing party in the case asks the court to reconsider the initial ruling either as a whole or on parts of the outcome.

It is typical that the permission, or leave, of the court is required for an appeal to proceed. This permission is typically sought from the court immediately after the judgment of the case has been confirmed, although an application can be made to the court where the party wishes for an appeal to be heard. This requires an application to be made to the court within 21 days of the original judgment and a fee is payable for raising the appeal.

The basis for an appeal to the county court is such that the appellant should only seek to bring an appeal if there is a real chance of a successful outcome or if the matter demonstrates a compelling rationale for an appeal to be heard. It should be noted that appeals are centred upon the decision that has been given in the original hearing – an appellant is appealing the decision of the court. They are therefore not retrials and therefore do not require new evidence to be adduced or new witnesses called.

CPR 52.21 confirms that:

> The appeal court will allow an appeal where the decision of the lower court was –
>
> (a) wrong; or
> (b) unjust because of a serious procedural or other irregularity in the proceedings in the lower court.

6.5 The High Court

The High Court is the third highest court in the UK. The court deals with civil cases, such as high value matters allocated to the Multi-Track, and appeals from the lower courts. The High Court is based at the Royal Courts of Justice in London with the central court supported via a series of district registries that are located throughout England and Wales.

The High Court comprises three divisions:

- The King's Bench Division.
- The Chancery Division.
- The Family Division.

All High Court Judges may sit in any of the three divisions, and they administer both under the law and under the equitable principles. In practice, though, judges are more typically assigned to specific divisions and even specific work within each division.

6.5.1 King's Bench Division

The King's Bench Division is the largest of the three divisions of the High Court. The Division is primarily responsible for claims for damages, injunctions and non-payment of debt matters all largely under the auspices of the CPR.

Within the umbrella of the King's Bench Division, sit a number of specialist courts including the Administrative Court, the Admiralty Court, the Commercial Court, Circuit Commercial Courts and the Technology and Construction Court.

These specialist courts are designed to deal with specific types of cases.

The Administrative Court

The Administrative Court has both a Civil and a Criminal Jurisdiction. The primary focus of the court concerns the exercise of public power. Through the process of judicial review, the court reviews the decisions of public bodies. This includes challenges that are made to the decisions of government ministers, applications under the principle of habeas corpus, coronial law matters, extradition appeals and decisions on planning matters.

The Commercial Court

The Commercial Court operates under CPR Part 58 and resolves business disputes of all kinds, excluding those of high value or complexity, which are issued via the Admiralty and Commercial Registry. Predominant court activity involves matters of finance, insurance, banking, arbitration and mercantile cases.

The Admiralty Court

The Admiralty Court deals with shipping and maritime disputes in tandem with the Commercial Court. Whilst the Commercial Court deals with more generalised contractual disputes, such as the high value matters that flow from shipping delays, the Admiralty Court deals with topics such as collision, salvage, towage, wages and pilotage. The business of the Admiralty Court is governed by CPR Part 61.

The Technology and Construction Court

The Technology and Construction Court handles a wide range of disputes that are implied by the court title. The court deals with building disputes; engineering disputes; claims that relate to the design, supply and installation of computers; and claims that relate to the quality of goods sold or hired and the work done.

6.5.2 Chancery Division

The Court of Chancery came into existence as a court of equity. The purpose of the court was to mitigate the harshness and inequity of the common law via a series of equitable principles, and these concepts continue today.

The most common types of cases that are dealt with in the Chancery Division relate to disputes involving property, business and land as well as the equitable concept of trusts. The division also considers disputes that are commercial in nature, competition claims, probate disputes and issues of intellectual property.

Within the Chancery Division there are also several specialist courts that deal with matters of patents, business insolvency and personal insolvency and bankruptcy.

6.5.3 Family Division

Prior to 2014, family cases would be dealt with as part of the standard business of the mainstream civil and Magistrates' courts. However, the impact of the Crime and Courts Act 2013 and the Children and Families Act 2014 was to transfer much of the family law caseload to a dedicated Family Court. This change in approach to family matters had the impact of lessening the role of the Family Division.

The Family Court structure recognises the highly emotive and specific nature of the work that is required in resolving family disputes that can involve the protection of children, contentious divorce proceedings, matters involving domestic violence and the provision of legal safeguards in matters of adoption. This is achieved via a range of measures including special training for the judiciary involved in family cases.

More complex family cases may end up in the Family Division of the High Court. It is also the venue for consideration of issues of specific societal or international significance such as cases of international child abduction, forced marriage and female genital mutilation.

6.5.4 Appeals From the High Court

Appeals against the outcome of a hearing in a county court or a High Court are usually dealt with by the Court of Appeal Civil Division. The Court of Appeal is the second most senior court in England and Wales, and the process of appeals is governed by CPR, Part 52.

Rule 52.6 states that:

Permission to appeal may be given only where –

(a) the court considers that the appeal would have a real prospect of success; or
(b) there is some other compelling reason for the appeal to be heard.

The same rule continues stating that orders to appeal can be restricted with limits placed upon the issues that will be considered by the Court of Appeal and/or conditions can be placed upon any appeal that a party may wish to bring.

The procedure for bringing an appeal before the Court of Appeal Civil Division is subject to a number of stages.

The first step requires strict compliance with the relevant time constraints for commencing an appeal. Appellants will usually have 21 days to appeal against a county court or High Court decision, but this is extended to 28 days in appeals that result from a decision of the Upper Tribunal. A seven-day time limit applies in a range of matters including when an appellant seeks to appeal a decision of the High Court refusing permission to apply for a planning statutory review at an oral hearing.

The second step is to ensure that an appeal with prospects of success is directed to the correct location. For example, in a small claims matter the likely next step involves an appeal to a High Court Judge prior to any appeals reaching the Court of Appeal. It is also important to ensure that permission to appeal has been granted.

If leave to appeal has been granted by a lower court or tribunal then the next step is to ensure that an appeal bundle is sent to the Court of Appeal. The contents of the bundle will vary according to the nature of the appeal but will likely include:

- An 'appellant's notice' that will provide an overview of the appellant's basis of appeal.
- A 'grounds of appeal' that documents the appellant's reasons for bringing the appeal before the court.
- A 'skeleton argument' that will outline the arguments that the appellant wishes the court to review in considering the appeal.
- A sealed copy of the decision that the appellant wishes the court to enact, should the appeal be successful.

The bundle should be provided in triplicate to the Court of Appeal and an additional copy should be provided for each respondent to the action.

If the appeal is judged to meet the tests outlined in CPR Part 52, then the appellant will be required to submit a core bundle to the court that contains all relevant documents. This should be paginated and ordered with a view to ensuring that the court can easily follow the appellant's case.

It should be noted that fees are payable to the court for the appeal.

When a lower court has not granted leave to appeal, an appellant can petition the Court of Appeal directly by completing the relevant forms and appeals pack.

Once again, three copies of the form and grounds of appeal will need to be submitted to the Court of Appeal, and an extra copy will be needed for each of the respondents to the appeal.

Should the Court of Appeal refuse permission to appeal then the appeal cannot continue further.

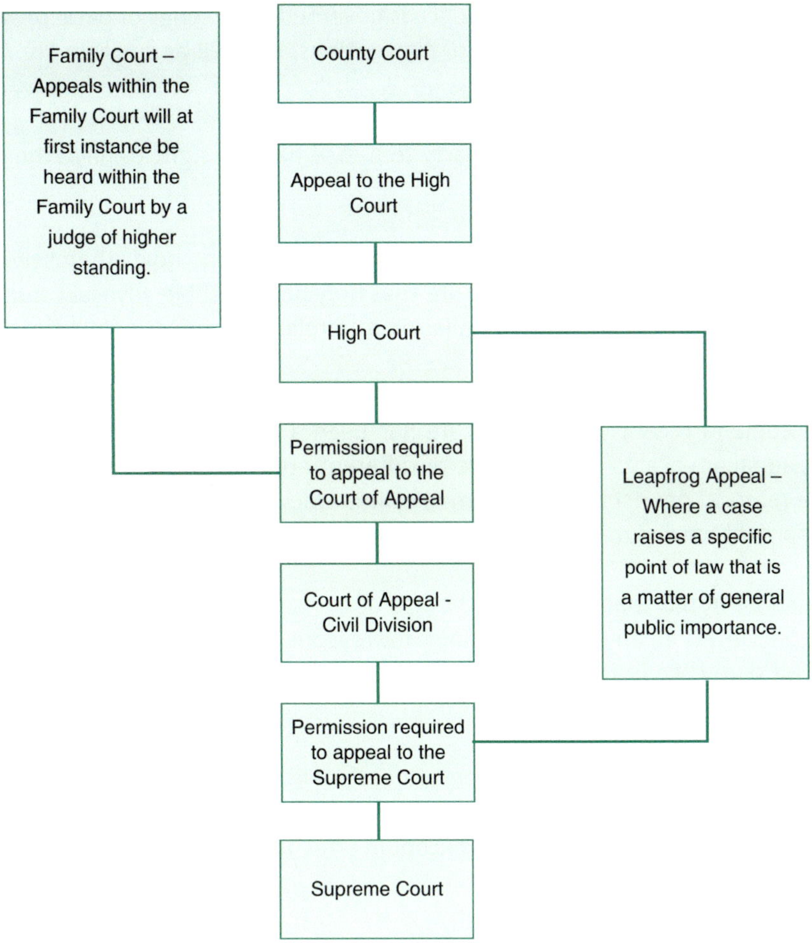

Figure 6.1 The Civil Appeals system

Where the appeal involves judicial review or results from the decision of a tribunal then specific provisions apply, as outlined with CPR, Part 52.

As an aide to reviewing this topic, Figure 6.1 represents the Civil Appeals system.

6.6 Rights of Audience

The starting point for consideration of the concept of 'rights of audience' is contained within the Legal Services Act 2007.

Within the Act, rights of audience are defined as the right 'to appear before and address a court, including the right to call and examine witnesses.' In other words, it is the right to be heard within the court by a judge.

The basis of asserting rights of audience is governed via a series of basic presumptions that are cited within a range of conventions, the CPR and within Pre-Action Protocols.

The first presumption is that any party to a case has the right to have their case put orally to the court via an advocate.

This is followed by the presumption that any individual who holds themselves out as a professional advocate must ensure that they hold suitable advocacy qualifications, supported by appropriate regulation and relevant professional protection – such as indemnity insurance.

It is notable in recent years that there has been a drive towards the removal of professional advocates from a range of different areas of law. An example would be the removal of costs from the small claims track in personal injury cases. This development has led to the rise of the litigant in person.

It should be noted that as well as the use of costs factors as a means to expand self-representation, any party to a claim for reasons of finance or due to a wish to put their own case in their own words, can make representations to the court to have the right of audience.

Finally, it is possible to utilise a non-professional advocate, such as a McKenzie Friend, to speak on your behalf. However, courts are often reluctant to allow this category to have a right of audience except in unusual circumstances.

6.7 Tribunals

Tribunals are specialist courts that are designed to run alongside the traditional courts with the aim of providing a forum for the multitude of legal issues that are generated each year. They are a vital part of the process, as without tribunals, the court system would quickly grind to a halt under the sheer volume of work.

Within the tribunal system, judges and members hear cases on a wide range of topics including employment, immigration, tax and asylum matters. Within the structure there also exists an appeal structure that is provided by the Upper Tribunal and the Employment Appeal Tribunal, in which decisions of the lower tribunals can be appealed.

The operation of tribunals is governed by the Tribunals, Courts and Enforcement Act 2007. The Act followed on from the creation of the Tribunals Service, as part of the Department for Constitutional Affairs in April 2006. Through the legislation, a single Tribunals Service was established to administer the work of 27 different types of tribunals. These can broadly be considered under three headings:

6.7.1 Local Authority Tribunals

Under the auspices of Local Authorities, there exists a range of tribunals that cover matters ranging from school exclusions through to the First-tier Tribunal for Special Educational Needs and Disability.

6.7.2 Governmental Tribunals

The Valuation Tribunal for England provides an example of a tribunal service that is run via a government department – the Ministry of Housing, Communities and Local Government. The Valuation Tribunal is an independent judicial body that deals with appeals about the level of Council Tax and non-domestic or business rates.

6.7.3 HM Courts and Tribunals Service Administrated Tribunals

HMCTS Tribunals represent the largest and most significant segment with tribunals grouped into two tiers: the First-tier Tribunals and the Upper Tribunals, and these elements are also further subdivided into a number of Chambers. Chambers have variations in the range of their jurisdiction with some relating to the whole of the United Kingdom, others relating to just England, just Wales or just Scotland. These Chambers are also divided into a range of bodies.

The seven Chambers of the First-tier Tribunal are as follows:

- War Pensions and Armed Forces Compensation Chamber.
- Social Entitlement Chamber.
- Health, Education and Social Care Chamber.
- General Regulatory Chamber.
- Tax Chamber.
- Immigration and Asylum Chamber.
- Property Chamber.

The First-tier Tribunals deal with a wide range of different legal matters from consideration of MP's Expenses appeals and Applications for people detained under the Mental Health Act 1983 through to disputes regarding Universal Credit and appeals against notices issued by the Information Commissioner.

The First-tier Tribunals sit with tribunal judges and other members, presided over by the Senior President of Tribunals.

Appeals against decisions of the First-tier Tribunal are generally made to the Upper Tribunal. The Upper Tribunal again consists of a number of Chambers including:

- Administrative Appeals Chamber.
- Tax and Chancery Chamber.
- Immigration and Appeals Chamber.
- Lands Chamber.

The Upper Tribunal has the primary role of reviewing and providing rulings on appeals that arise from the First-tier Tribunal. It should be noted that any further leave to appeal will tend to be made from the Upper Tribunal to the Court of Appeal, as outlined in CPR Part 52.

6.8 The Senior Courts

The Senior Courts of England and Wales came into existence as the 'Supreme Courts of Judicature' with the enactment of the Judicature Acts of 1873 and 1875. Since that point, the Senior Courts have been renamed by the Supreme Court Act 1981 (now the Senior Courts Act 1981) to become the 'Supreme Court of England and Wales.' The enactment of the Constitutional Reform Act 2005 had the effect of changing the title again. This time they became the 'Senior Courts of England and Wales.' This step was taken as a means to create space for the new Supreme Court of the United Kingdom, which replaced the House of Lords as the highest court in the land.

The Senior Courts of England and Wales comprise:

- The Court of Appeal.
- High Court of Justice.
- Crown Court.

In the next section, we will focus on the role of the Court of Appeal.

6.8.1 The Court of Appeal

The Court of Appeal exclusively deals with matters that are subject to appeal from either the lower courts or tribunal. The Court of Appeal is divided into two divisions with the Civil Division hearing appeals from the High Court, the county court and from some of the tribunals. The Criminal Division hears appeals that are directed from the Crown Court.

It is important to note the position that the Court of Appeal holds within the court structure. On the one hand, decisions from the Court of Appeal are such that they bind all of the lower courts. However, it is noted that the Supreme Court hears appeals from the Court of Appeal and therefore binds the Court of Appeal with its decisions.

It is typically the case that permission to appeal to the Court of Appeal is required prior to a case making it to this level. This can either be via a lower court granting permission or via a direct application to the Court of Appeal itself. Regardless of the route to bring an appeal, it should be noted that the process is subject to restrictive time constraints. An appellant would typically need to lodge the relevant notice within 21 days of the original decision, and this must be accompanied by the relevant grounds of appeal.

If permission to appeal is granted, then the matter will usually be heard before a three-person court. The process is one where this is not a further trial of the original evidence, nor is this usually the opportunity to introduce new evidence into proceedings. Instead, the Court of Appeal seeks to review the original case decision where the matter involves a question of law.

6.9 The Supreme Court

The Supreme Court is the final court of appeal in the UK for civil cases and for criminal actions from England, Wales and Northern Ireland. The focus of the Supreme Court is the consideration of cases that have the greatest importance to the public or to the effective operation of the constitution. The decisions tend to have bearing across the whole of the populace.

The Supreme Court predominantly hears appeals from the Court of Appeal, the Scottish Court of Session and the Court of Appeal in Northern Ireland. However, it should be noted that the process of a 'leapfrog' appeal can result in a case jumping from the Divisional or High Courts directly to the Supreme Court.

The usual process for appeal involves a direct application to the Supreme Court for the relevant permission. At this point the matter will be considered by an appeals committee that comprises three Justices of the Supreme Court. Once again, strict time limits apply with appeals needing to be raised within 28 days of the date of the Court of Appeal order. It should be noted that permission is granted sparingly and tends to be restricted to cases that require a ruling upon an important point of legal principle.

As a practical point, a dissenting judgment in the Court of Appeal tends to be a positive point when considering whether to bring an appeal.

Should the matter be considered for appeal then it will typically be heard by five Justices of the Supreme Court, although it should be noted that as little as three and as many as nine could be involved.

6.10 Judicial Committee of the Privy Council (JCPC)

The Judicial Committee of the Privy Council (JCPC) is the court of final appeal for matters that originate within UK overseas territories, such as the Falkland Islands, the Cayman Islands and Gibraltar, and Crown dependencies, such as the Bailiwick of Jersey, the Bailiwick of Guernsey and the Isle of Man.

The committee was originally established in 1833 to hear appeals that had previously been heard under the King-in-Council protocol.

Once again, the matters that are addressed by the JCPC relate to matters of public importance. When a case is brought before the JCPC, it will typically be heard by a panel of five judges. The judges are collectively referred to as The Board and it is The Board who produce a report which, by convention, is always accepted by the King-in-Council as judgment.

The work of the Committee is governed by the Judicial Committee (Appellate Jurisdiction) Rules 2009 which cover matters such as permission to appeal the conduct of hearings.

Chapter 6 Revision Points

Within this chapter we have considered a number of aspects of the SRA SQE1 syllabus on the Legal System of England and Wales. This includes consideration of the hierarchy of courts, matters of jurisdiction and the venues to which appeals can be directed.

This has included an overview of the role of the county court, a consideration of the High Court and its numerous divisions, a review of the concept of rights of audience and consideration of both tribunals and the more senior courts of the UK and its territories.

It is important to check your knowledge using the following Multiple Choice Questions.

Multiple Choice Questions

Question 1

Whilst working in a restaurant, a person slips on water that had accumulated due to a leaking fridge-freezer (that had been left ajar), suffering a broken arm. The individual spent six months in recovery and was also unable to work during this period. A solicitor, after seeking advice from Counsel, has valued the general and special damages at £64,000. The factual matrix of the accident is abundantly clear, due to the person being injured in the course of his employment, resulting from the negligence of his co-worker and employer. There is an admission of liability due to CCTV footage, and the quantum is not likely to be disputed.

In terms of commencing proceedings, which court would be the most appropriate?

A. Employment Tribunal.
B. The Chancery Division of the High Court.
C. The Divisional Court.
D. The county court.
E. The Family Division of the High Court.

Question 2

An electrician has developed a solar battery system for home and businesses that results in electricity being used in fractional amounts, thus saving substantial costs to the User. He has managed this by being innovative in the use of the battery packs, power optimisers and storage inverters. He has now patented the solar battery system, and given the current climate, seeks to profit substantially from the sale of these solar battery systems. He estimates that profits in year one would be circa £600,000. Unfortunately, his solar battery pack has been infringed by a local company, who have sold 15000 of these batteries.

The electrician seeks to commence court proceedings with the aim of seeking a remedy and the destruction of the infringing battery packs, in which court can this be done?

A. The Court of Appeal (Criminal Division).
B. The King's Bench Division of the High Court.
C. The Chancery Division of the High Court.
D. The county court.
E. The Patent's Court.

Question 3

You are seeking leave to appeal a decision that has been made in the Court of Appeal (Civil Division).

Which of the following courts have the power to grant permission to appeal?

A. The Court of Appeal and the Supreme Court.
B. The Court of Appeal only.
C. The Supreme Court only.
D. The Court of Justice.
E. The Court of Appeal and the House of Lords.

7 Criminal Courts

7.1 SQE1 Syllabus

The SQE1 syllabus requires that you have an understanding of the criminal justice system in England and Wales and of the complex interaction between a range of governmental and private organisations. This network manages the process from crime, to accusation, through the court process to possible conviction and then on to the management and rehabilitation of offenders.

7.2 Chapter Overview

In this chapter we will be focussing on the operation of the courts in a criminal context, along with consideration of the criminal justice and criminal appeals processes.

7.3 The Hierarchy Within the Criminal Courts

It is important to note that the Criminal Courts operate on a distinct basis from the Civil Courts considered previously, with the Criminal Courts existing to hear prosecutions. These prosecutions follow a charge being levied, usually by the Crown, which will state that an offence has been committed deserving of criminal sanction and punishment.

The Magistrates' courts are the lower court within the criminal court process, and they will hear matters relating to summary offences and some triable either-way offences. They are the venue where all prosecutions begin, even if this is simply to immediately refer the offence to the Crown Court for onward consideration.

The Crown Courts are responsible for hearing all indictable offences, those either-way offences that have been sent by the Magistrates' Court and appeals of the decisions of the Magistrates' Court.

From the two initial criminal courts there exists a range of higher courts that deal with appeals. These include the Administrative (Divisional) Court of the King's

DOI. 10.4324/9781003435525-13

Bench Division of the High Court, the Court of Appeal (Criminal Division) and then the Supreme Court.

In addition to these courts, it should also be noted that there exists a number of other courts as well. These include:

- The Youth Courts – who deal with criminal defendants under the age of 18.
- The Judicial Committee of the Privy Council – who deal with appeals from the Commonwealth.
- Coroners Courts – who deal with matters where an inquest is required into the death of an individual.

7.4 The Criminal Justice Process

Criminal justice is a process, involving a series of steps that commence with the commission of a crime. This leads to criminal investigation and eventually ends with the release of a convicted offender from custody. As part of our consideration of this area we will consider the roles of the Police, the Crown Prosecution Service, the use of rules of criminal procedure and the courts.

7.4.1 The Police

It is only appropriate to start the process of considering criminal justice with an evaluation of the role of the police.

The police services in the UK are organised around two distinct concepts, the Office of Constable and the police force.

Office of Constable

Every officer of the police in England and Wales, irrespective of role or rank, holds the title of Constable and it is from the title of Constable that each individual who serves in the police derives their powers in regard to detection, prevention and the investigation of crime.

These powers ensure that officers can prevent crime, monitor criminal activity, oversee the conduct of communities, maintain public order and in the enforcement of the law through arrest, interview, investigation and then through working with the Crown Prosecutors to ensure that charges are brought. The police are also involved within the court process, predominantly as witnesses for the prosecution.

Police Force

In turn, every police officer is a member of a police force, and it is the role of the police force to provide an organisational structure through which crime can be prevented and investigated and criminal evidence gathered. At present there are 43 police forces in England and Wales.

With the considerable powers that are provided to both police officers and police forces it is important to note that they are part of an overarching structure that ensures that their performance is monitored.

This has been given considerable press coverage following the conviction of serving officer Wayne Couzens following the murder of Sarah Everard.

The Independent Office for Police Conduct (IOPC)

The Independent Office for Police Conduct (IOPC) is the complaints watchdog for police services in England and Wales. They have the role of investigating the most serious complaints against the police and also review the conduct of individual officers. The office also sets the standards by which each individual police force should handle complaints made directly to them.

In 2021/22 the IOPC logged over 75,000 complaints against the police and this represented an 11% increase on the previous year.

7.5 The Process of Investigation

Figure 7.1 shows the typical process that will be employed in the investigation of a criminal offence.

Instigation Criminal investigation can commence via a wide range of different actions. These include reports made to the police by members of the public, agency referral and intelligence that has been recorded with regards to criminal activity. These are referred to as reactive investigations.

Proactive investigations commence via police activity including crime pattern analysis, operational intelligence assessment, subject analysis and tactical assessment.

Initial Investigation The initial investigation phase of the process will require officers to undertake a range of activities including crime scene management, record keeping, initial searches and initial interviews. Priority should be given to the preservation of life, the preservation of the crime scene, the security of evidence and the identification of victims and suspects.

Investigative Evaluation The first decision point requires officers to make an initial determination as to whether to proceed onward with the case, seek further evidence prior to looking to progress the matter or whether the matter should cease at this point as having no cause of action. It should be noted that even where a case

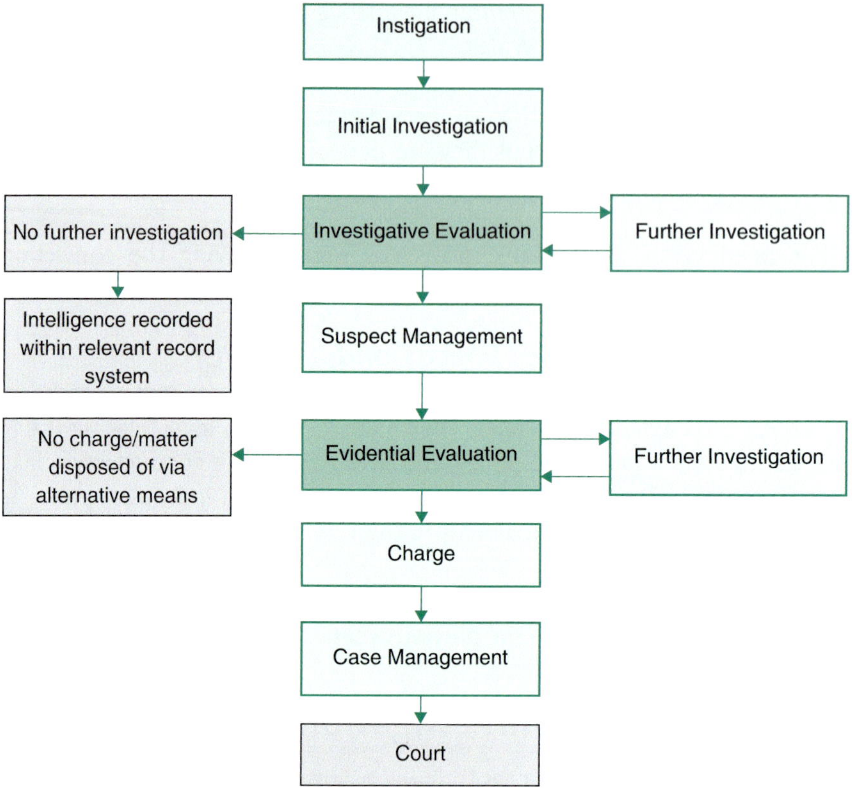

Figure 7.1 The typical process of a criminal offence

is closed at this stage, all intelligence, evidence and information gathered should be recorded with a view to the prevention and detection of future crime.

Suspect Management Where the matter proceeds further through the process, the police are then required to follow Guidance 10A of Code C of the Codes of Practice to the Police and Criminal Evidence Act 1984. This states that where a person is suspected of involvement in the commission of crime, that the police must ensure that there are reasonable, objective grounds for this suspicion, based upon known facts.

As part of the suspect management process, investigations can be directed more specifically towards the individual and the evidence that is available against that person.

Evidential Evaluation The second decision point requires officers to make a further determination of the evidence available in the case. This is completed with a view to identifying whether the matter is such that there is no ongoing charge that can be brought, whether the matter is best suited to be disposed of via alternative means such as warning or fine, whether further investigation is needed prior to any decision, or whether the suspect should be charged with the offence.

Charge When an individual is charged with a criminal offence, legal proceedings are then underway against the suspect. The decision to charge an individual can be made by either the police or Crown Prosecution Service. However, in practice it will often be a combination of the two. Under the guidance appended to section 37A of the Police and Criminal Evidence Act 1984, the police hold the responsibility for ensuring that they have pursued all reasonable lines of inquiry with a view to ensuring that the prosecutor can make a well-informed decision that takes into account the evidence in favour of prosecution and the evidence that supports the defence.

Case Management Following charge the case then proceeds under the process outlined in the Criminal Procedure Rules. These will be considered in more detail later.

Court The matter will then reach the final stage of the process, the court hearing. This will provide an opportunity for the accused to enter a plea with regards to the charge. If the accused pleads guilty then the defendant is convicted of the crime, and they will be sentenced. In 2022, 76% of defendants prosecuted entered a guilty plea at court.

If the accused pleads not guilty then the matter proceeds to trial.

7.5.1 The Crown Prosecution Service

The Crown Prosecution Service (CPS) prosecutes criminal cases that have been investigated by predominantly the police. It is important to note that the CPS are a wholly independent body who render their decisions on cases without interference by either the police or the government.

The overriding duty of the CPS is to ensure that the right person is prosecuted for the right offence, with the aim of bringing offenders to justice.

The Code for Crown Prosecutors outlines the two-stage legal test that is employed in the reaching of decisions about whether to prosecute an individual.

Stage one asks the prosecutor to consider whether there is enough evidence against the suspect to provide a realistic prospect of conviction.

In essence, the prosecutor is evaluating whether it is more likely than not that a court will find a defendant guilty, based upon the available evidence. This requires an evaluation of the reliability, credibility, and evidential value of the case against the defendant.

If the matter passes the stage one test, then we proceed to consider stage two.

Stage two asks whether it is in the public interest to prosecute.

The prosecutor now completes a review of the matter to ascertain public interest in prosecution. This requires consideration of the seriousness of the offence, the magnitude of the harm caused to the victim or to wider interests, such as a local community. Factors such as age and maturity will also be considered, and this is particularly relevant in matters involving young offenders.

Once the defendant has been charged it is the role of the CPS to then prepare the case and present it at court.

7.5.2 The Criminal Procedure Rules

The Criminal Procedure Rules are the rules established to regulate the conduct of matters placed before the criminal courts. They apply in the Magistrates' courts, the Crown Court, the Court of Appeal and to matters within the High Court, for example extradition appeal cases.

The rules are divided into sections that cover all aspects of the criminal trial process. They are available via legislation.gov.uk and should be read alongside the relevant Criminal Law Practice Directions.

As with the Civil Procedure Rules, the Criminal Rules also start with an overriding objective which states that:

> The overriding objective of this procedural code is that criminal cases be dealt with justly.

The rules then outline the factors that ensure that a case is dealt with in a just manner. The rules also cover areas such as case management, case progression, disclosure, directions and trial preparation.

The rules are also supplemented by a range of statutory instruments that have the purpose of ensuring that the rules are regularly updated. These changes are often the subject of legal commentary.

7.5.3 The Magistrates' Court

As highlighted previously, the first venue for a criminal trial will be the Magistrate's Court.

Matters within the court are presided over by Magistrates, and these individuals are the 'justices of the peace.' Those who sit as Magistrates tend to be local people who volunteer for the role, and it should be noted that no formal legal qualifications are needed prior to taking on the role, although a training programme is provided that typically includes both court and prison visits.

The legal aspect of a Magistrates' Court hearing comes from clerks to the court who provide both legal and procedural advice.

When a case before a Magistrates' Court involves more complex or legally challenging matters, it would be typical for a District Judge to preside.

Over 95% of all criminal cases are dealt with at the Magistrates' Court with the court having jurisdiction over summary only offences and some either-way offences.

The maximum sentence on conviction for one offence heard by the Magistrates' Court is six months and the minimum custodial term that can be applied is five days. However, where an either-way offence is heard by the Magistrates' Court, it is within the powers of the court to commit the case to the Crown Court for sentencing.

The court can also utilise a range of alternative penalties upon those who are found guilty before the court and this could include fines, compensation, anti-social behaviour orders, restraining orders and sexual offence prevention orders.

The trial process within the Magistrates' Court commences with the defendant being formally identified and then being required to confirm their plea.

The case will then proceed with the prosecutor formally opening the prosecution case by summarising the allegations that have been made against the defendant. The case will then proceed with the prosecution calling witnesses to provide their evidence. The defence team will have the opportunity to seek to weaken the prosecution case via the process of cross examination.

When the prosecution case is complete, the defence will then have the opportunity to put forward their case on behalf of the accused. Again, witnesses can be called, and this could include the defendant themselves.

With the two cases outlined to the court, the prosecutor will then give a closing statement that summarises the prosecution case and will remind the court of the key evidence that has been heard before the court during the trial. The defence will then give their closing statement.

With the respective cases outlined, the Magistrates', or District Judge, will retire to consider the evidence that has been presented and will return with the verdict of the court.

Should the accused be cleared of the charge, they will be formally acquitted by the court and the case will be closed. If the prosecution has successfully made out their case, then the court will move to the final stage of the court process, namely sentencing.

Sentencing can take place immediately or could be delayed whilst a pre-sentence report is compiled by the probation service.

7.5.4 The Crown Court

The Crown Court has the role of dealing with the more serious criminal cases including matters of murder, rape and armed robbery. In addition, the Crown Court also has jurisdiction over appeals that are made from either a conviction or a sentence that have been handed down in the Magistrates' Court.

The Crown Court, as well as dealing with the more serious indictable only offences and appeals, will also deal with sentencing decisions that have been transferred from the Magistrates' Court and will deal with either-way offences that the Magistrates' Court feel would be better heard in the Crown Court.

Cases in the Crown Court commence with an initial hearing at which the defendant is expected to enter a plea to the charges that have been brought against them. It is only if the defendant enters a not guilty plea that the matter then proceeds to a full trial. The trial process commences with the court setting a timetable for the progression of the case, and this will include a plan to ensure that the legal process is observed and pertinent evidence heard.

It is important to note that when a case is to procced to full trial it can feature in either the fixture or the warned list.

A fixture, as the name suggests, is a fixed date upon which the trial will commence. The warned list provides a date range during which the trial will begin. There is no fixed date; it will simply be a date during that court window. If it is not possible to accommodate a case within the warn period, then the matter falls into a next warn period that may be as much as a number of months later.

The trial process in the Crown Court commences with the attendance of advocates for the defendant and the prosecution. With the parties in attendance, the judge will then make an initial ruling upon the legal arguments that are to be put forward by the advocates.

Subject to no disagreements in the legal arguments, the first role of the court is to manage the process of selecting a jury of 12 people.

Jury Selection

It is the responsibility of the Crown Court to ensure that sufficient members of the general public are summonsed to attend the court to hear a case. The process of summoning individuals to the court is an automated process completed within a central office of the court with names being selected from those listed on the electoral register.

Once an individual receives a summons, they are required by law to attend for jury service or to notify the court immediately if they are unable to attend as required.

Fines of £1000 can be levied against an individual who fails to respond to the summons.

The usual commitment that a jury is required to give is for a period of ten working days, but this can be extended beyond this period as the case requires.

As an example, the 2023 case of *R v Letby*[1] went on for a period of ten months. In the final determination the judge, Mr Justice James Goss, informed the jury that it had 'been a distressing and upsetting case' and they would be excused from serving on juries in the future.

Once the jury is sworn in, it is the role of the prosecution advocate(s) to outline the case and to call witnesses to provide evidence. The prosecution witnesses will, in turn, be cross examined, by a defence barrister. When all witnesses for the prosecution have been called and given evidence, the defence barrister will then seek to rebut the prosecution case via the calling of defence witnesses and the process of cross examination is reversed.

When all evidence has been heard by both sides, the jury will be addressed in the form of closing statements from both sides. The judge will then provide a summary to the jury and will provide guidance on their legal responsibilities, which may include guidance as to the relevant law.

The jury will then retire before returning to the court with a decision as to the defendant's guilt or innocence.

If the decision of the jury is not guilty, then the defendant will be discharged from the court. If a guilty verdict is returned, then the court may seek to impart the sentence immediately. However, it is often more common for proceedings to be adjourned to allow for pre-sentencing reports to be prepared and then considered.

7.6 The Criminal Appeals Process

The process of criminal appeals is such that it is important to note the initial differences between criminal appeal and those within the civil court process.

The first key difference is simply one of outcome. Namely, in a criminal case the matter is often tied to the freedom of an individual. As the stakes are likely to be high, the assumption of the appeals process is one where the defendant should be given the opportunity to apply for an appeal with a view to establishing their innocence. The other key difference is in the differential that exists between the two

1 *R v Letby* [2023].

parties. Where it is considered appropriate to allow a defendant every opportunity to appeal their conviction, the right to appeal is restricted on the prosecution side of the case. This restriction tends to limit prosecution appeals to those matters where an appeal is required from the decision of a lower court regarding a point of law.

7.6.1 Appeals From Magistrates' Court

If a defendant feels that they have been wrongly convicted in the Magistrates' Court, then they have an automatic right to appeal. The appeal would typically be heard in the Crown Court, and the appeal must be lodged at the court within 15 business days of sentencing.

Appeals can be brought against either the conviction, the sentence or against both. Typical grounds on which to bring an appeal include:

- Evidence should have been excluded from the case.
- Excluded evidence should have been considered.
- New evidence has come to light that has a material bearing on the case.
- The interpretation of the law was incorrect.
- The trial process was procedurally unfair.
- The Magistrate or District Judge simply got it wrong.

To lodge an appeal, a defendant simply needs to a file the 'Notice of Appeal against Conviction (or against Conviction and Sentence) with the Magistrates' Court.

The appeal process is one where the entire case is reheard before a Crown Court Judge, sitting with two Magistrates' who are independent of the original case decision.

Again, the prosecution and defence teams present their evidence, and they are able to call either the same witnesses, more witnesses or less – should they choose to do so.

Once the case has been heard, the decision of the court is one of a simple majority between the judge and the two Magistrates.

The outcome of an appeal will be either that the Crown Court allows the appeal, meaning that the verdict is then changed to not guilty, or the appeal could be dismissed, and the original verdict will then stand.

In exceptional circumstances, the court may be asked to hear an appeal following a guilty plea being entered at the Magistrates' Court. In these circumstances, the case is not reheard. Instead, the appeal will focus on whether the original guilty plea should stand. If the court decides that there is some reason to disregard the original guilty plea then the case is remitted back to the Magistrates' Court for the defendant to enter a not guilty plea, prior to a trial then taking place.

In addition, there are two alternatives to taking an appeal to the Crown Court. A defendant can seek to have the case re-opened at the Magistrates' Court or they can bring an appeal under a process known as an 'appeal by way of case stated.'

The re-opening of a case at the Magistrates' Court is contained within section 142(2) of the Magistrates' Courts Act 1980. This process allows the Magistrates' Court to direct that a defendant can have a trial heard again but with a new Magistrate or District Judge presiding.

This occurs where the court feels that a rehearing of the case would be in the interest of justice with examples being where perhaps a defendant was not in attendance at the original hearing or where all parties agree that an error has occurred in the completion of the original trial. This process does not require an application to be brought in 15 working days, but rule 44.3 of the Criminal Procedure Rules does state that an application needs to be made 'as soon as reasonably practicable.'

Appeal by way of case stated is an option that allows a defendant to appeal directly to the High Court, or to a specialist court within the King's Bench Division of the High Court – typically the Administrative Court.

The appeal by way of case stated process can used by either the defence or prosecution and is reserved for where guidance is required on a matter of law.

7.6.2 Appeals From the Crown Court

If a defendant believes that they have been wrongly convicted in the Crown Court, they can seek permission to appeal against the conviction to the Court of Appeal (Criminal Division). It should be noted that there is no automatic right of appeal.

The defendant has 28 days to make an application to appeal either a conviction after a jury trial or in circumstances where a guilty plea has been entered at the Crown Court.

Again, this route of appeal is only available for the defendant in very limited circumstances, such as where it has been discovered that there has been interference with or intimidation of a juror or a witness.

The appeals process follows a multi-stage process, outlined in section 18 of the Criminal Appeals Act 1968 and in Part 26 and Part 39 of the Criminal Procedure Rules:

1) Form NG Conviction – An Application for Permission to Appeal against Conviction – along with the Grounds of Appeal must be served within 28 days of conviction on the Registrar of Criminal Appeals at the Criminal Appeal Office.

2) It should be noted that the 28-day time frame is from conviction and not from sentencing.
3) Any application outside of the 28-day period requires the defendant to apply for an extension of time, and this must include the reasons behind the request.
4) The Grounds of Appeal document must identify, on a point-by-point basis, each ground that the defendant seeks to rely upon. These must include concise arguments to support the grounds and the overall appeal request.
5) It should be noted that the appeals process may be commenced whilst an individual is in custody. An appellant can therefore also enclose an Application for Bail Pending Appeal.
6) Upon receipt of the appeal documentation, a single judge will review the grounds and will make the decision as to whether to allow the matter to proceed to the Court of Appeal for a hearing. This decision will be based upon whether the grounds of appeal demonstrate sufficient merit to proceed.
7) If the grounds are considered sufficient, then the matter will proceed to a hearing at the Court of Appeal.
8) If the permission to appeal is refused, the defendant can seek to renew the application with the grounds then being considered by the full Court of Appeal.

If the matter does proceed to the Court of Appeal, it will be heard by the full Court of Appeal at a formal hearing heard by at least three judges, usually comprised of a Lord Justice of Appeal and two High Court Judges.

The judges will consider the grounds of appeal that have been submitted and will hear submissions from both the appellant and the prosecution.

Under Part 1, sections 1 to 8 of the Criminal Appeal Act 1968, the Court of Appeal has the power to either quash the conviction as being unsafe, to substitute a verdict for an alternative offence, to order a retrial or to dismiss the appeal.

7.6.3 Appeals to the Supreme Court

Appeals to the Supreme Court can be made either from the Court of Appeal or directly from the Administrative Court. Such an appeal can only be made where permission has been provided either by the court in question or directly by the Supreme Court itself.

Appeals to the higher court only occur rarely as the only matters that the Supreme Court consider are those that involve a point of law that is of general public importance. Recent examples can be found in the cases of *R v Jogee* [2016] UKSC 8 (joint enterprise) and *R v Golds* [2016] UKSC 61 (diminished responsibility).

Once again, parties must comply with a 28-day deadline for applying for leave to appeal and it should be noted that either the defendant or prosecution can request permission.

7.6.4 Appeals to the Judicial Committee of the Privy Council

The Judicial Council of the Privy Council is the court of last resort regarding criminal appeals from countries within the Commonwealth. To bring an appeal to the Council requires permission to have been granted by the lower court whose decision the party seeks to appeal. Where the lower court refuses to grant leave to appeal then a party can make an application for permission directly to the Board.

As with the Supreme Court, matters before the Council tend to be such that they raise questions of great importance or relate to matters that offend the principles of natural justice.

Chapter 7 Revision Points

Within this chapter we have considered a number of aspects of the SRA SQE1 syllabus on the Legal System of England and Wales. This includes consideration of the hierarchy of criminal courts, matters of jurisdiction and the venues to which appeals can be directed.

This has included an overview of the role of the Magistrates' Court, a consideration of the role of the Crown and High Court, a review of appeals processes and consideration of the senior courts of the UK and its territories.

It is important to check your knowledge using the following Multiple Choice Questions.

Multiple Choice Questions

Question 1

You have prosecuted a defendant in the Magistrates' Court for common assault. On this occasion, the Magistrates found the defendant not guilty. You are of the opinion that the Magistrates have made an error in interpreting and applying the law. You wish to appeal.

To which court can you apply?

A. You can appeal direct to the Court of Appeal (Criminal Division).
B. By way of case stated to the Crown Court, and in the instance your application is refused, you can appeal to the Supreme Court.
C. By way of case stated to the Administrative (Divisional) Court of the King's Bench Division of the High Court, and in the instance your application is refused, you can appeal to the Supreme Court.
D. By way of case stated to the Administrative (Divisional) Court of the King's Bench Division of the High Court, and if the appeal is granted the defendant will be retried at the Crown Court.
E. By way of case stated to the Administrative (Divisional) Court of the King's Bench Division of the High Court, and if the appeal is allowed it will be held in the Court of Appeal (Criminal Division).

Question 2

A jury at the Crown Court has found a man guilty of assault occasioning actual bodily harm. There was a guilty plea, no aggravating factors and a number of mitigating factors. The judge has decided to jail the man for five years. The defence feel the sentence is too harsh and not befitting the circumstances of the man's case.

Even the prosecution were somewhat surprised at the sentence, but from their perspective think it is fair.

The man wants to appeal.

Which would be the most appropriate?

A. The prosecutor can appeal to the Court of Appeal on the basis the sentence is too harsh.
B. The defence can appeal against conviction to the Court of Appeal on the basis the verdict is unsafe.
C. The defence can appeal to the Court of Appeal as an unjust precedent has been set.
D. The defence can appeal by way of case stated to the Queen's Bench Division of the High Court.
E. The defence may appeal against sentence to the Court of Appeal if the sentence is manifestly excessive.

Question 3

A man has been arrested and charged with the murder of his brother in the Midlands. The man has denied murder and wishes to contest it as he acted in self-defence. You have been tasked with explaining the next steps.

Which of the following would represent the best advice?

A. If the man is convinced to plead guilty, there will be no need for a jury trial, and he will be sentenced at the first hearing at the Magistrates', which will result in a more lenient sentence.
B. The case will be sent for trial to the Crown Court, where due to the inexperience of the circuit judge a legal advisor will be able to assist in a judicial capacity.
C. The case will be sent for trial to a suitable Crown Court venue either in Birmingham or nearby, and the man will be tried in front of a jury.
D. The local Magistrates will listen to the prosecution's evidence, and then make an order for the case to be transferred to the Crown Court.
E. The man would like for the trial to be heard in a court in London, given its proximity to Cheapside, where he was born, and the constitution allows for the same.

PART

6

Legal Services

8 Regulating Legal Services

Within the pages of the Law Society Gazette each week there is a specific section of the publication that is given over to disciplinary matters that have been considered regarding legal professionals. Each week those in the legal profession will often consider these pages as a means to consider whether competitors, colleagues or former academic peers have fallen foul of the multitude of rules and regulations that govern the provision of legal services within England and Wales.

It is therefore important to consider these rules and regulations as a means to understand the framework in which both individual legal professionals and legal practices operate.

8.1 SQE1 Syllabus

The role of legal professionals is such that we are often tasked with roles of trust and responsibility at the most vital times in the life of individuals, businesses and other organisations.

Whether we are advising on matters of medical negligence at birth, the instigation of trust arrangements for those of minority, employment matters during an individual's career, during the purchase of property or even on matters after an individual has passed away, the role of the legal advisor is one of trust and confidence.

If trust and confidence within legal service providers is not present then it is impossible to have an effective legal system.

The SQE1 syllabus requires an understanding of the regulatory role of the SRA and the principles that underpin the risk-based approach to regulation.

8.2 Chapter Overview

Within this chapter we will analyse how regulatory systems have been created to ensure that all individuals who work within the legal services sector apply the highest standards of integrity and professionalism at all times.

DOI: 10.4324/9781003435525-15

8.3 Defining Legal Services

If we are to consider the regulatory process that applies to legal services, it is important to firstly consider what constitutes a legal service.

If we were to consult a dictionary, we would typically find definitions of legal services that consider the notion of a lawyer working for a client. However, a general definition is always going to be problematic as this would always need further clarification – for example, what is meant by the concept of working?

It is therefore important to note that there exists no set definition of the term, beyond it being considered a general overarching theme under which the roles of advisor, helper and representative would sit.

This broad starting point ensures that a multitude of differing roles are captured by the regulatory framework that is upheld by the Solicitors Regulation Authority (SRA).

For example, all solicitors registered in England and Wales, Registered European Lawyers, and Registered Foreign Lawyers who work within legal practice, private practice, sole practice or within the charitable sector are all subject to authorisation and regulation by the SRA.

In addition, many of those who support the functions of the legal service are also subject to SRA regulation including all paralegals, claims handlers, administration staff, trainee solicitors and managers who work within those law firms. In addition, every authorised law firm also comes under the regulatory framework.

8.4 The Solicitors Regulation Authority (SRA)

The SRA was established in January 2007 following the Legal Services Act 2007. However, it can be observed that there have been many previous methods of regulatory control upon the legal profession with evidence showing that as far back as 1275 'deceit or collusion' by lawyers was forbidden within the Statute of Westminster.

Between 1825 and 2007 the role of legal service regulator fell to the Law Society. However, this was deemed to be a conflict of interest as the Law Society also held the role of being both the representative body for the profession and the organisation tasked with protection and enhancing the reputation of the profession.

Following the Clementi review of 2004, legislation was enacted that set out the requirements of the regulator. Section 1(1) of the Legal Services Act 2007 sets out the 'regulatory objectives' as:

a) Protecting and promoting the public interest.
b) Supporting the constitutional principle of the rule of law.
c) Improving access to justice.
d) Protecting and promoting the interests of consumers.
e) Promoting competition in the provision of services within subsection (2).
f) Encouraging an independent, strong, diverse and effective legal profession.
g) Increasing public understanding of the citizen's legal rights and duties.
h) Promoting and maintaining adherence to the professional principles.

The SRA sets out its purpose as being 'to protect the public by ensuring that solicitors meet high standards, and by acting when risks are identified.'

The protection of the public aspect of regulation is underpinned by the SRA Principles and the SRA Code of Conduct.

The SRA Principles state the expectations that are placed upon those who are regulated by the authority. The principles are as follows:

You act:

1) in a way that upholds the constitutional principle of the rule of law, and the proper administration of justice.
2) in a way that upholds public trust and confidence in the solicitors' profession and in legal services provided by authorised persons.
3) with independence.
4) with honesty.
5) with integrity.
6) in a way that encourages equality, diversity and inclusion.
7) in the best interests of each client.

The SRA Code of Conduct follows the principles whilst setting out the ways in which regulated individuals should behave in respect of their clients. The Code of Conduct achieves this by setting out the standards of professionalism that the SRA, and vicariously the general public, expect from those authorised.

The Code of Conduct is available online.

It should be noted that in addition to the SRA, the 2007 Act also established the Legal Services Board.

The Legal Services Board is an independent body responsible for overseeing the regulation of the organisations that regulate solicitors, barristers, legal Executives, licensed conveyancers, patent attorneys, trademark attorneys, costs lawyers, notaries and chartered accountants. The Board also oversees the Office for Legal Complaints and the Solicitors Disciplinary Tribunal.

8.5 Authorisation

As the approved regulatory body for the legal sector, the SRA holds responsibility for the authorisation of firms (meaning recognised bodies, licensed bodies and recognised sole practices) and of individuals (as practising solicitors, Registered European Lawyers and Registered Foreign Lawyers). Authorisation allows firms and individuals to carry out what are referred to as 'reserved legal activities.'

8.5.1 Reserved Legal Activities

Historically, there was much of the role of the lawyer or barrister that was reserved solely for those who held that status. The reason for reserving such activities solely for those with professional status and authorisation was one of public protection – namely, an individual would have to have a specific level of qualification, experience, standing and professional insurance cover to provide that service to the general public.

Within section 12 (1) (a)-(f) of the Legal Services Act 2007, there are six specific activities that are reserved, with only individuals and business that are authorised by an approved regulatory able to carry out those activities.

The activities are as follows:

a) The exercise of a right of audience – this is the right to appear before and to address a court on a legal matter. This would also include the ability to call and examine witnesses.
b) The conduct of litigation – this is the right to issue proceedings before the courts of England and Wales and can include the commencing, prosecuting or defence of proceedings. It should be noted that the right would also extend to any functions required to complete the conduct of litigation. An example would be the entering of appearances to actions.
c) Reserved instrument activities – these typically relate to matters involved in the process of conveyancing as they refer to transactions that involve real and personal property. This could therefore involve property sale, long term leases or liens. It should be noted wills, short-term leases, powers of attorney and stock transfers outside of a trust instrument are not included.
d) Probate activities – this is the right to prepare documents that enable the grants of probate of letters of administration to be obtained. Similarly, this includes the right to contest the grant to another.
e) Notarial activities – this is the right to certify and authenticate documents that were previously reserved via the Public Notaries Act 1801.
f) The administration of oaths – this is the power to administer an oath.

It should be noted that whilst the Legal Services Act outlines the listed activities as requiring authorisation, section 19 of the Act also outlines the activities for which exemptions can also be applied. An example would be where a court grants a right of audience to a lay person or McKenzie Friend who can then address the court on the matter at hand.

8.5.2 Firm-Based Authorisation

Reserved activities are such that they must usually be provided through an authorised firm. Firms become authorised by the SRA when they have completed the application process and the SRA have deemed that they meet the standards for authorisation.

In the past there was considerable criticism of the SRA for the length of time that was required for a firm to progress from application to authorised status with the whole process taking up to six months to complete. However, much work has been done to speed up the process with applications now taking as little as four weeks to complete.

The process of gaining authorisation commences with form FA1, which requires applicants to provide information on areas such as who the compliance officers will be, who the firm managers will be, who owns the business and who is authorised as a signatory for the organisation. The form also requires identification of responsibility for key protections such as anti-money laundering officers.

As well as identifying the key personnel, the SRA also requires information on sources of funding, interest rates, types of work undertaken and any linked businesses with a view to assessing the viability of the proposed business.

Accompanying information about the firm will also be a number of FA2 forms that provide information on the individual post holders. This will focus on their proposed roles, their professional status, their experience, employment history and background information including business interests.

In assessing viability, the SRA will expect to see the company's business plan, financial forecasts and projections, risk assessment and business continuity plans and also standard governance documents such as shareholder agreements.

These requirements are set out within the SRA Authorisation of Firms Rules.

Rule 8 specifies requirements regarding the appointment of compliance officers. These officers must be approved by the SRA to hold one of two key offices – namely the Compliance Officer for Legal Practice (COLP) and the Compliance Officer for Financial Affairs (COFA).

8.5.3 Individual Authorisation

The SRA Authorisation of Individuals Regulations set out the requirements, placed upon an individual who wishes to be authorised by the SRA. The regulations were most recently amended to reflect the changes to the SRA requirements that came into effect with the introduction of the Solicitors Qualifying Examination (SQE).

The regulations set out that to be eligible for admission individuals must:

- Have successfully and satisfactorily passed an assessment which is designed to assess your competence against the prescribed competences for solicitors and is conducted by an assessment organisation appointed by the SRA for the purpose;
- you hold a degree or qualifications or experience which the SRA is satisfied are equivalent to a degree;
- you have completed qualifying work experience which meets the requirements of regulation 2; and
- demonstrate the character and suitability to be a solicitor.

The next stage of the process involves the individual being admitted to the roll of solicitors. Once admitted, the person's name is added to a publicly available list that is maintained by the SRA.

The third stage of the individual authorisation process requires the individual to apply for a practising certificate. The certificate, once issued, allows the individual to offer legal services. The practising certificate renewal process takes place between the 1st and 31st of October each year, with renewal required on a bulk or individual basis each year.

For year 2023/24 the practising certificate renewal fee was £337.

Once a practising certificate has been issued, the solicitor is then authorised and regulated by the SRA to carry out reserved legal activities.

The SRA Authorisation of Individuals Regulations also outline the process that is required for both Registered European Lawyers and Registered Foreign Lawyers to become authorised.

8.6 Professional Indemnity Insurance

The SRA Indemnity Insurance Rules state that all SRA authorised firms are required to hold valid professional indemnity insurance (PII).

Rule 3.1 of the SRA Indemnity Insurance Rules states: 'an authorised body must take out and maintain professional indemnity insurance that provides adequate and appropriate cover in respect of current or past practice taking into account any alternative arrangements the body or its clients may make.'

The purpose of this requirement is to ensure that clients of the legal practice have financial protection in place should the standard of service provided by the solicitor fall below an acceptable standard, causing loss to the client. Examples would include where the solicitor has been negligent in their advice to the client or where there has been a breach of duty in the conduct of legal proceedings.

Professional Indemnity Insurance is designed to cover the payment of such liabilities with a view to helping to maintain confidence in the profession.

PII is a requirement for all new SRA authorised firms prior to the commencement of legal services. Policies are renewed on an annual basis with firms required to demonstrate that cover is in place at the time when practising certificate renewal is completed.

8.7 Unregulated Providers

It should be noted that not all legal services are subject to regulation under the Legal Services Act 2007.

A range of activities that are fundamental to the legal system in England and Wales are regulated via alternative means. Examples include Immigration Advisors who are regulated via the Office of the Immigration Services Commissioner rather than via the SRA. The same applies to Insolvency Practitioners who are subject to the rules imposed by the Insolvency Practitioners Association. It should also be noted that Claims Management enterprises, although often heavily involved in access to legal work, are not regulated by the SRA but are instead under the auspices of the Financial Conduct Authority.

Similarly, there are whole areas of the legal sector that are entirely unregulated including will writing, family law advisory services and employment law advice.

Chapter 8 Revision Points

Within this chapter we have considered a number of aspects of the SRA SQE1 syllabus on the provision of legal services in England and Wales. This includes consideration of the process of authorisation, the regulatory framework and the legislation that underpins the operation of a legal service provider.

It is important to check your knowledge using the following Multiple Choice Questions.

Multiple Choice Questions

Question 1

Two friends who are not learned or legally qualified wish to open a firm offering clinical negligence services to hospital users where they work in the IT department. They have noted a gap in the market.

Which of the following best describes the position regarding the regulatory requirements which will apply to the proposed firm?

A. The firm does not need to be authorised by the SRA.
B. The firm must be authorised by an approved regulator.
C. The firm must be authorised by the Law Society and SRA jointly.
D. The firm must be authorised by the Legal Services Board.
E. Authorisation for the firm is dealt with by the Legal Services Act 2009.

Question 2

The Solicitors Regulation Authority authorised a solicitor to provide legal services.

Which of the following best describes the effect of this?

A. As they have been authorised, no further action is required from the regulatory body.
B. All reserved legal activities can be provided by a solicitor.
C. The SRA will only regulate *reserved* legal activities.
D. Any work undertaken by the solicitor is regulated by the Legal Services Board.
E. All legal services provided by the solicitor will be regulated by the SRA.

9 Overriding Legal Obligations

9.1 SQE1 Syllabus

It is important to note that the role of a solicitor is not only to act as a key aspect of the operation of the law but is also to ensure that the law is upheld with regards to their own obligations. There are therefore a range of legal obligations that require consideration as part of the SQE and these include the Equality Act 2010, the Money Laundering, Terrorist Financing and Transfer of Funds (Information on the Payer) Regulations 2017 (SI 2017/692) and the Proceeds of Crime Act 2002.

9.2 Chapter Overview

The SQE1 syllabus requires an understanding of a diverse range of areas from the Equality Act 2010 through to the criminal sanctions that can apply in matters of money laundering. Solicitors must have an awareness of how their role can also interact with financial services regulations.

9.3 Equality Act 2010

It is important to note that the Equality Act 2010 was very much a consolidating piece of legislation. In fact, the Act brought together over a hundred separate pieces of legislation under the auspices of just one prevailing Act of Parliament.

Prior to this step, the unfair treatment of an individual was covered by one of a number of pieces of legislation including the Equal Pay Act 1970, the Sex Discrimination Act 1975, the Race Relations Act 1976 and the Disability Discrimination Act 1995.

The notion of bringing together equality legislation under one Act was to ensure that fair treatment was managed consistently regardless of the type of discrimination that was experienced.

The approach taken to this area is largely contained within the civil law, although there are a number of discriminatory acts that can lead to criminal sanction such as inciting racial hatred and some extreme forms of harassment. With the matter dealt with via civil means there is flexibility within the approach that stops short

DOI: 10.4324/9781003435525-16

of an overall ban on discrimination. Instead, the legislation outlaws certain types of discrimination and it is these areas that are often key when looking at the operation of a legal practice.

Through the establishment of a set of protected characteristics the law operates to provide recourse to those subject to discrimination in many forms.

The Act operates by allowing an individual to take action against discrimination through a claim for redress. This can be via the county courts for most matters with employment matters dealt with within the Employment Tribunal. Where an individual is successful in their claim they are entitled to remedy in the form of damages. However, it should be noted that equitable remedy also exists with possible outcomes including injunctions, declarations and in employment matters the requirement for reinstatement or re-engagement.

9.3.1 Protected Characteristics

Section 4 of the Equality Act 2010 states that the following are protected characteristics:

- Age.
- Disability.
- Gender reassignment.
- Marriage and civil partnership.
- Race.
- Religion or belief.
- Sex.
- Sexual orientation.
- Pregnancy and maternity.

Age

Age discrimination occurs where a person is treated unfairly because of their age, or because they are part of particular age group. This is outlined within section 5 of the Act.

It should be noted that age is covered differently than other parts of the Equality Act. These differences reflect the view that in some circumstances a difference in treatment based on age can be justified. Examples where the justifiable defence has been raised have included in matters of health and safety, where an individual's welfare requires protection and where the aim of an activity is for people of particular age groups to be involved.

Disability

Disability discrimination occurs when an individual is treated unfairly due to a reason that is connected with either a physical or mental impairment that has a substantial and long-term adverse effect on their day-to-day activities. This is defined within section 6 of the Act and is further qualified through Schedule 1 which defines the effect of an impairment as long-term if:

a) it has lasted for at least 12 months,
b) it is likely to last for at least 12 months, or
c) it is likely to last for the rest of the life of the person affected.

The Schedule also confirms that specific conditions require consideration as a disability, for example HIV.

The disability provisions within the Act have been subject to criticism as they do set a high threshold through the requirement for a substantial and long-term effect to be suffered.

Gender Reassignment

A person has the protected characteristic of gender reassignment if they are proposing to undergo, are undergoing, or have undergone a process (or part thereof) for the purpose of reassigning the person's gender by changing their physiology or associated attributes.

The provisions are contained with section 7 of the Act, and it is important to note that whilst disability provisions apply a high threshold, the provisions within section 7 apply without the individual being under medical supervision with regards to the reassignment process.

Marriage and Civil Partnership

Section 8(1) of the Act provides that:

(1) A person has the protected characteristic of marriage and civil partnership if the person is married or is a civil partner.

Marriage refers to a person who is legally married under the Marriage Act 1949 and includes same-sex couples. Civil partner refers to an individual who is a civil partner under the Civil Partnership Act 2004. It is important to note that this only applies to same-sex couples.

The protections afforded to individuals here do not include those who cohabit, single people, divorces, fiancées or any alternative form of personal relationship standing.

Race

Race is defined within section 9 of the Act and includes:

a) Colour.
b) Nationality.
c) Ethnic or national origin.

The definition is very wide and can lead to individuals being afforded multiple levels of protection where they are members of several different racial groups.

The protection that is afforded under section 9 arises where an individual is treated less favourably because of their colour, nationality, ethnicity or national origin. Despite the wide remit afforded to race, it is important to note that it has been the subject of a number of key cases including *Mandla v Dowell Lee* [1983] 2 AC 548, *Ealing LBC v Race Relations Board* [1972] AC 342 and in the case of *Commission for Racial Equality v Dutton* [1989] IRLR 8 which ruled that gypsies constituted an ethnic group.

Religion or Beliefs

It is important to note that section 10 of the Act is far less prescriptive than the approach taken to the area of race. Within section 10 the terms religion and belief are not defined other than to say that any religion or philosophical belief and an absence of either of these is covered.

The approach ensures that a religion, no matter how small or how well known will be given protection under the Act provided that it has a clear structure and belief system.

A belief can also be either a religious belief, such as observed in the case of *Eweida v United Kingdom* [2013] ECHR 37, [2013] IRLR 231 or could be a philosophical belief.

The case of *Grainer Plc and Others v Nicholson* [2009] UKEAT/0219/09ZT outlined a series of steps to consider as to whether a belief was protected. The judgment states that a protected belief must:

1) Be genuinely held.
2) Be a belief and not an opinion or viewpoint based on current information.
3) Be a belief as to a weighty and substantial aspect of human life and behaviour.
4) Attain a certain level of cogency, seriousness, cohesion and importance.
5) Be worthy of respect in a democratic society, not be incompatible with human dignity and not conflict with the fundamental rights of others.

Using these criteria, it was held in the case of *Conisbee v Crossley Farms Ltd and others* [2019] ET/3335357/2018 that vegetarianism did not meet the criteria to be a protected characteristic.

However, in the case of *Casamitjana Costa v League Against Cruel Sports* [2020] ET/3331129/2018 the judge held that ethical veganism is capable of being a philosophical belief.

Sex

The Equality Act 2010 provisions that relate to sex are designed to regulate unfair conduct between men and women.

For the purposes of the Act, under the general provisions relating to equality in matters of sex, a person's sex is determined by their biological sex as recorded on their birth certificate. In 2023, the Minister for Women and Equalities sought advice from the Equality and Human Rights Commission on the definition that should be used with regard to the Equality Act, and this is an ongoing matter.

The Act generally makes it against the law to discriminate against an individual because of the protected characteristic of sex. However, there are conditions set out in the Act that do allow, where conditions are met, for services to be provided either exclusively to one sex, or differently depending on the sex of the service user or entirely separately to each sex.

Sexual Orientation

Sexual orientation is defined under section 12 of the Act as a sexual orientation towards either persons of the same sex, persons of the opposite sex or persons of the same and the opposite sex.

The Act states that you must not discriminate against an individual because:

- They are heterosexual, gay, lesbian or bisexual.
- You believe that someone has a particular sexual orientation – this is also known as discrimination by perception.
- The individual is connected to someone who has a particular sexual orientation – this is also known as discrimination by association.

It should be noted that the Act takes a wide view with regards to what may be considered to be the expression of sexual orientation, and this can include an individual's appearance or even the places that they chose to visit.

Pregnancy and Maternity

Under section 4 of the Equality Act 2010, pregnancy and maternity are protected characteristics. However, these characteristics are treated in an entirely different fashion under the Act with some elements of the Act specifically excluded and other more specific protections included.

Under the Act, it is unlawful to discriminate against an individual because they are pregnant, because they are suffering with a pregnancy related illness, have recently given birth, are breastfeeding or are taking or have requested maternity leave.

An individual is able to gain protection under the Act if the discriminatory act falls within the protected period. The protected period commences when an individual becomes pregnant and continues until the end of the period of maternity leave through either returning to work, or leaving your current employment. In circumstances where maternity leave does not apply, for example for agency workers, the protected period ends two weeks after giving birth.

Following consideration of the protected characteristics, the next stage is to then consider the types of conduct that the Act prohibits.

9.3.2 Prohibited Conduct

The Act outlines a range of different types of unequal treatment. These include direct discrimination, indirect discrimination, discrimination that specifically arises from disability, harassment and victimisation. Each will be considered in turn.

Direct Discrimination

Under section 13(1) of the Act, direct discrimination occurs where:

A person (A) discriminates against another (B) if, because of a protected characteristic, A treats B less favourably than A treats or would treat others.

In other words, due to a protected characteristic, an individual has been treated in a less favourable manner than someone else would have been in the same situation. The nature of direct discrimination is such that it is plain and obvious that a disadvantage has occurred.

However, the matter can become a more complicated consideration when applied to matters such as equal pay and equal rights across different roles within an organisation.

With a view to providing a framework for assessment there exists a three-stage test:

Stage one – Identify a comparator.

The starting point is the identification of someone who is in the same or a similar enough situation to the individual but that does not possess the protected characteristic. This already introduces a potentially subjective element as we need to ensure that we can identify what is similar enough. The starting point here is to note that we are not seeking an identical situation but instead one where there are at least some common points raised in both circumstances that would allow for the protected characteristic to be identified as the basis of the unequal treatment. So, if for example, an employer who allows a Christian employee time off to attend events related to their religious belief would be a suitable comparator should a Muslim employee of the same company be refused time off for Friday prayer.

The matter of a comparator becomes even more subjective where there is no real person to whom a comparison can be made. In these circumstances, a hypothetical comparator can be used. As an example, should a pregnant employee make a mistake at work that leads to a customer complaint and because of that complaint the employer dismisses the employee. If this is a situation that has not occurred before then it would be possible to review how previous complaints had been dealt with to identify if the dismissal was based on the protected characteristic.

Stage two – Has there been less favourable treatment?

The test here is to be able to identify that the treatment that has been afforded to the individual has been less favourable than the treatment that was given to the comparator. However, once again there are subjective elements to consider here with regards to what amounts to less favourable treatment. The Act deals with this by having a broad concept of less favourable treatment that simply requires the individual to show that a disadvantage has been suffered. This ensures that the test is objective in nature. It should also be noted that disadvantage can take many forms and does not require a tangible or material loss to have been incurred. Similarly, there is no need to demonstrate malice in the actions of the perpetrator, although it should be noted if there is a clear motive for the discrimination then this can be reflected in any damages awarded in the case.

Stage three – Is there a protected characteristic?

The final stage of the process is the need to demonstrate that the individual's protected characteristic was the cause of the discrimination. However, it is important to note that the protected characteristic does not have to be the sole cause of the unfair treatment, but it must be the main influence.

Indirect Discrimination

Indirect discrimination is outlined within section 19 of the Act as:

1) A person (A) discriminates against another (B) if A applies to B a provision, criterion or practice which is discriminatory in relation to a relevant protected characteristic of B's.
2) For the purposes of subsection (1), a provision, criterion or practice is discriminatory in relation to a relevant protected characteristic of B's if –
    a. A applies, or would apply, it to persons with whom B does not share the characteristic,
    b. it puts, or would put, persons with whom B shares the characteristic at a particular disadvantage when compared with persons with whom B does not share it,
    c. it puts, or would put, B at that disadvantage, and
    d. A cannot show it to be a proportionate means of achieving a legitimate aim.

So whilst direct discrimination requires an overt or obvious act that cannot be justified, indirect discrimination is a much less obvious act that discriminates against an individual when a policy, practice or rule is put in place that applies to the whole populace, but that same policy, practice or rule has an adverse impact upon those who share one of the protected characteristics.

It is often the case that matters of indirect discrimination can have justifiable intent and in cases where the action is a proportionate aim of achieving a legitimate aim there can be a solid defence raised to any claim that is brought.

As an example, should an employer advertise a job role that specifies a minimum height requirement, where a person's height has no bearing on the successful applicant's ability to carry out the role. It would be likely that the requirement may well be indirect discrimination as it would discriminate disproportionately against women, some minority ethic groups, etc.

It is important to note that the protected characteristics of pregnancy/maternity are considered under direct discrimination and not the indirect category.

For all other protected characteristics, the process of considering an indirect discrimination claim again requires a series of steps to be considered.

The starting point is to consider whether the basis of the discrimination is a practice, policy or rule. It is important to note that this could be an arrangement, a criterion, a condition, a specified qualification or select provisions. This clearly provides a wide range of different basis on which a claim could be founded. The important common characteristic is that the basis applies to everyone in the same way.

For example, if a health club had a rule that stated that all employees were required to work on Saturdays, this would clearly be an arrangement that would apply equally to all. However, a policy of this kind would undoubtedly discriminate against a Jewish person who observes the Sabbath.

The next step is to identify whether the practice, policy or rule has actually led to disadvantage to you as an individual as you can only challenge on the basis of indirect discrimination if you have been personally impacted.

It is then required to show that others who share the protected characteristic are also disadvantaged in a similar fashion by the practice.

Discrimination Arising From Disability

Whilst both direct and indirect discrimination pathways are available to those who are disabled, it should be noted that under section 15 of the Equality Act 2010, there is a specific provision that relates to disability discrimination.

Under section 15:

A person (A) discriminates against a disabled person (B), if A treats B unfavourably because of something arising in consequence of B's disability.

This is a wide definition that enhances the statutory rights available to disabled people.

In demonstrating a cause of action, we are required to consider what amounts to unfavourable treatment under section 15. It is important to note that the term is given its normal everyday meaning – namely that you are in a worse position because of the way that you have been treated.

Unlike with actions under the direct discrimination heading, in matters arising from disability, there is no need to compare the situation with a comparator. Instead, an individual needs to show that they have been treated unfavourably because of something to do with their disability.

Examples include the need to take regular rest breaks, the need for time off to attend medical appointments, the need for special equipment to be provided to support you in your job role, such as specialist software or a specific type of office chair, or the need for an assistance animal.

Similar to our consideration of indirect discrimination, it should be noted that it is possible to justify less favourable treatment, if it can be shown that it is a proportionate means of achieving a legitimate aim. It should also be noted that the discrimination arising from disability can only occur where the accused is, or should reasonably have been, aware that the individual had a disability.

Harassment

Under section 26 of the Equality Act 2010:

1) A person (A) harasses another (B) if –
   a. A engages in unwanted conduct related to a relevant protected characteristic, and
   b. the conduct has the purpose or effect of –
      i. violating B's dignity, or
      ii. creating an intimidating, hostile, degrading, humiliating or offensive environment for B.
2) A also harasses B if –
   a. A engages in unwanted conduct of a sexual nature, and
   b. the conduct has the purpose or effect referred to in subsection (1)(b).
3) A also harasses B if –
   a. A or another person engages in unwanted conduct of a sexual nature or that is related to gender reassignment or sex,

b. the conduct has the purpose or effect referred to in subsection (1)(b), and
c. because of B's rejection of or submission to the conduct, A treats B less favourably than A would treat B if B had not rejected or submitted to the conduct.

Within section 26, it is noted that any evaluation of conduct that may amount to harassment requires the perception of the victim, the whole circumstances of the case and whether it is reasonable for the conduct to have that effect to be taken into account.

Victimisation

Section 27 of the Equality Act 2010 details the provisions relevant to victimisation.

1) A person (A) victimises another person (B) if A subjects B to a detriment because –
   a. B does a protected act, or
   b. A believes that B has done, or may do, a protected act.
2) Each of the following is a protected act –
   a. bringing proceedings under this Act;
   b. giving evidence or information in connection with proceedings under this Act;
   c. doing any other thing for the purposes of or in connection with this Act;
   d. making an allegation (whether or not express) that A or another person has contravened this Act.

It is noted that the term detriment is not provided with a specific definition within the Act. Instead, the courts have taken the view that the term detriment is any act which has the effect of creating a disadvantage to an individual.

It should also be noted that section 27 protection does not require the victim to have a protected characteristic; the provision is open to all.

9.3.3 Solicitors' Obligations as Service Providers

It is often easy to consider the role of those who provide legal services as the representatives of parties to an action under the provisions of the Equality Act 2010.

However, it is important to note that the provisions of the Act apply to legal service providers directly in their role as service providers.

Under Part 3 of the Equality Act, and more specifically section 29:

1) A person (a 'service-provider') concerned with the provision of a service to the public or a section of the public (for payment or not) must not

discriminate against a person requiring the service by not providing the person with the service.

2) A service-provider (A) must not, in providing the service, discriminate against a person (B) –
   a. as to the terms on which A provides the service to B;
   b. by terminating the provision of the service to B;
   c. by subjecting B to any other detriment.
3) A service-provider must not, in relation to the provision of the service, harass –
   a. a person requiring the service, or
   b. a person to whom the service-provider provides the service.
4) A service-provider must not victimise a person requiring the service by not providing the person with the service.
5) A service-provider (A) must not, in providing the service, victimise a person (B) –
   a. as to the terms on which A provides the service to B;
   b. by terminating the provision of the service to B;
   c. by subjecting B to any other detriment.
6) A person must not, in the exercise of a public function that is not the provision of a service to the public or a section of the public, do anything that constitutes discrimination, harassment or victimisation.
7) A duty to make reasonable adjustments applies to –
   a. a service-provider (and see also section 55(7));
   b. a person who exercises a public function that is not the provision of a service to the public or a section of the public.

As the duty applies to legal practices it is important to ensure an awareness of the duty to make reasonable adjustments, unlawful behaviour under section 29 and the concept of vicarious liability.

Duty to Make Reasonable Adjustments

Whilst the impact of the Equality Act tends to be considered in terms of retrospective action – after the event or inequality has occurred. It is noted that provisions that relate to discrimination impose positive duties upon the individual that ensure that steps are taken to ensure that potential discrimination is avoided at the outset.

Under section 20 of the Act:

The duty comprises the following three requirements.

1) The first requirement is where a provision, criterion or practice of A's puts a disabled person at a substantial disadvantage in relation to a relevant

matter in comparison with persons who are not disabled. There is a duty to take such steps as is reasonable to avoid the disadvantage.

2) The second requirement applies, where a physical feature puts a disabled person at a substantial disadvantage in relation to a relevant matter in comparison with persons who are not disabled. There is a duty to take such steps as is reasonable to avoid the disadvantage.
3) The third requirement applies, where a disabled person would, but for the provision of an auxiliary aid, be put at a substantial disadvantage in relation to a relevant matter in comparison with persons who are not disabled. There is a duty to take such steps as is reasonable to ensure the provision of the auxiliary aid.

Where the first or third requirement relates to the provision of information, the steps which it is reasonable for A to have to take include ensuring that in the circumstances concerned the information is provided in an accessible format.
Under section 21:

1) A failure to comply with the first, second or third requirement is a failure to comply with a duty to make reasonable adjustments.

In evaluating whether a service provider has discriminated against a disabled person the courts utilise the test of substantial disadvantage. In this context substantial is defined as being more than minor, more than trivial and this represents a relatively low threshold to reach.

Unlawful Behaviour

As part of the section 29 provisions within the Equality Act, it is important to note that whether you practise as a sole practitioner, in a firm of solicitors or via an Alternative Business Structure that, as a legal service provider you are under a duty to comply with the Act.

So, when dealing with a service user, a solicitor must not:

- Discriminate against or victimise a prospective or current client by refusing to provide a service.
- Discriminate against or victimise a prospective or current client as to the terms upon which the service is provided.
- Discriminate against or victimise a prospective or current client by unreasonably terminating the provision of the service.
- Discriminate against or victimise a prospective client or current client by subjecting the client to any other detriment.
- Harass a prospective or current client.

So should a solicitor refuse to continue to provide a service to a client based upon that client's sexual orientation, then this would amount to clear discrimination based upon a protected characteristic.

Vicarious Liability

Section 109 of the Equality Act 2010 ensures that an employer may be held vicariously liable for the unlawful acts of their employees committed in the course of their employment. This liability is affixed to the employer even if the employee's acts were undertaken without the firm's approval and even if the employer is not aware of the employee's act.

The main defence that can assist an employer, in such a matter, is where the firm is able to show that they have taken reasonable steps to prevent the particular act of discrimination. This would only apply if the mitigation were undertaken prior to the discriminatory act. An example would be where an employer can demonstrate that they have provided to employees training that is appropriate to the matter at hand.

9.4 The Money Laundering, Terrorist Financing and Transfer of Funds (Information on the Payer) Regulations 2017 (SI 2017/692)

Money laundering is a process that is used by criminals to make it appear that the proceeds of criminal activity derive from a legitimate course.

With the role of a solicitor often requiring a significant number of financial transactions to take place between the solicitor and the client, legal practices are often particular targets for criminals seeking to launder money.

9.4.1 Purpose and Scope

On a simplistic level, money laundering involves the proceeds of criminal activity being passed to a legal practice, for example the payment of a deposit on a proposed property purchase. Those funds could be held by the legal practice for some period of time before being returned to the client when the sale does not proceed. The monies have in effect been laundered.

In reality, attempts at laundering money tend to be more complicated with the use of intermediaries and multiple transactions to obfuscate the true source of the funds.

The use of multiple small investments, multiple individuals and various parts of the legal process can make it difficult to trace the original source of the funds and therefore prosecute those involved in serious and organised crime.

When seeking to prevent money laundering activity it is important for legal practices to be aware of the three stages involved in a money laundering transaction.

Stage 1 – Placement.

This is where the cash proceeds from crime are used to purchase property, used to fund a retainer or are passed to the solicitor to hold for some future transaction.

Stage 2 – Layering.

At this point a single transaction would be easy to unravel and so the process begins of moving the money on multiple occasions to confuse the trail. This could involve the sale of property, a request to cease the intended legal action (and hence return the retainer) or the monies held could be returned to the client under the guise that the future purchase is not to continue. This cycle is then repeated with each iteration further covering the trail.

Stage 3 – Integration.

The final stage of the process is where the money is then utilised for a legitimate purchase/activity.

It should be noted that attempts to confuse and obscure the source of money can often cross jurisdictions and hence money laundering tends to be considered on global rather than national levels.

The introduction of the Financial Action Task Force provides a global response to matters of money laundering and the funding of terrorist activity. In the UK, the recommendations of the task force are implemented via the Money Laundering, Terrorist Financing and Transfer of Funds (Information on the Payer) Regulations 2017 (SI 2017/692).

The regulations impose a number of duties that are relevant to legal practice, these are as follows:

Regulation 18. –

1) A relevant person must take appropriate steps to identify and assess the risks of money laundering and terrorist financing to which its business is subject.

Regulation 19. –

1) A relevant person must –
    a. establish and maintain policies, controls and procedures to mitigate and manage effectively the risks of money laundering and terrorist

financing identified in any risk assessment undertaken by the relevant person under regulation 18(1);

b. regularly review and update the policies, controls and procedures established under sub-paragraph (a);
c. maintain a record in writing of –
    i. the policies, controls and procedures established under sub-paragraph (a);
    ii. any changes to those policies, controls and procedures made as a result of the review and update required by sub-paragraph (b); and
    iii. the steps taken to communicate those policies, controls and procedures, or any changes to them, within the relevant person's business.

2) The policies, controls and procedures adopted by a relevant person under paragraph (1) must be –
    a. proportionate with regard to the size and nature of the relevant person's business, and
    b. approved by its senior management.

Regulation 21.

1) Where appropriate with regard to the size and nature of its business, a relevant person must –
    a. appoint one individual who is a member of the board of directors (or if there is no board, of its equivalent management body) or of its senior management as the officer responsible for the relevant person's compliance with these Regulations;
    b. carry out screening of relevant employees appointed by the relevant person, both before the appointment is made and during the course of the appointment;
    c. establish an independent audit function with the responsibility –
        i. to examine and evaluate the adequacy and effectiveness of the policies, controls and procedures adopted by the relevant person to comply with the requirements of these Regulations;
        ii. to make recommendations in relation to those policies, controls and procedures; and
        iii. to monitor the relevant person's compliance with those recommendations.

Under Regulation 21, a legal practice must appoint a money laundering compliance officer who holds the overall responsibility for compliance with the regulations. In addition, a legal practice is also required to appoint a money laundering reporting officer. Within this role the officer holds responsibility for making suspicious activity reports to the National Crime Agency.

Regulation 24.

1) A relevant person must –
   a. take appropriate measures to ensure that its relevant employees are –
      i. made aware of the law relating to money laundering and terrorist financing, and to the requirements of data protection, which are relevant to the implementation of these Regulations; and
      ii. regularly given training in how to recognise and deal with transactions and other activities or situations which may be related to money laundering or terrorist financing.
   b. maintain a record in writing . . . . of the training given to its relevant employees.

Regulations 27 and 28.

Legal practices must take steps to verify the identity of their clients. This process must commence as soon as possible after initial contact between the client and the legal practice. The verification documents should then be retained on file for a period of five years.

9.4.2 Due Diligence Requirements

Due diligence is the process where a legal practice completes the required checks to identify a client. This process should be undertaken prior to the commencement of any business relationship between the client and the legal practice.

The Requirement for Due Diligence

Regulation 27 states that:

1) A relevant person must apply customer due diligence measures if the person –
   a. establishes a business relationship;
   b. carries out an occasional transaction that amounts to a transfer of funds within the meaning of Article 3.9 of the funds transfer regulation exceeding 1,000 euros;
   c. suspects money laundering or terrorist financing; or
   d. doubts the veracity or adequacy of documents or information previously obtained for the purposes of identification or verification.

Further guidance is provided via Regulation 28 which provides:

12) The ways in which a relevant person complies with the requirement to take customer due diligence measures, and the extent of the measures taken –
   a. must reflect –
      i. the risk assessment carried out by the relevant person under regulation 18(1);

    ii. its assessment of the level of risk arising in any particular case;
  b. may differ from case to case.

13) In assessing the level of risk in a particular case, the relevant person must take account of factors including, among other things –
  a. the purpose of an account, transaction or business relationship;
  b. the level of assets to be deposited by a customer or the size of the transactions undertaken by the customer;
  c. the regularity and duration of the business relationship.

Legal practices must therefore use differing types of due diligence dependent upon the type of client, the area of law and the anticipated risk of money laundering activity being present.

These are:

- Standard due diligence.
- Simplified due diligence.
- Enhanced due diligence.

Standard Due Diligence

As the title suggests, standard due diligence is the approach that is used with the majority of legal practice clients. The process involves the verification of a client's identity via a reliable and independent source such as a driving licence or passport. Where the client is a company, this would be achieved by the verification of the company via the company name, company number and registered place of business. It should be noted that for partnerships the process is completed by completing the required checks on the individuals who comprise the partnership.

Simplified Due Diligence

Again, as the title suggests, simplified due diligence takes a lighter touch approach to the verification process. This lighter form of diligence is permitted where the business relationship or the specific transaction is such that the risk of money laundering occurring is low. In circumstances where the client was a well-known company whose shares are listed on a regulated market, a solicitor is permitted to use the simplified approach to the due diligence process. In this example, simple confirmation of the company's listing would suffice.

Enhanced Due Diligence

Where the risk of money laundering is more significant than usual, the enhanced due diligence procedure would be enacted. Regulation 33 documents the circumstances where the enhanced process should be utilised. These are:

- Where the matter has been identified, by its very nature, as one where the risk of money laundering is high.
- Where the client is based in a nation that is considered high risk.

- Where the client is identified as a politically exposed person, or whom has a direct relationship with a politically exposed person.
- Where the client has provided false information or documentation and yet the legal practice proposes to continue with the transaction.
- Where the pattern of behaviour is such that it shows unusual characteristics within the transactions. This may be indicated by complexity, a lack of purpose in the transactions or where the level of, frequency of or parties to a transaction raise suspicion.

9.4.3 Reporting Requirements

It is a duty placed upon each solicitor that they report circumstances that are suggestive of money laundering activity. To ensure that this takes place, solicitors should be aware of the signs to look out for. The SRA guidance on the subject suggests the following:

- A client may be secretive, evasive or uncooperative.
  - The client may refuse to provide information, may avoid contact from the solicitor or is a known figure within the criminal fraternity or is connected to persons who are.
  - Where large cash deposits are made, particularly where the deposits are paid from unknown sources.
  - Unusual transactions or instructions.
- Erratic client behaviour such as an insistence on completing an ill-advised transaction or where undue haste is demanded.
- It is also important to consider how the client has come to use the solicitor in question. If the client and the solicitor are some distance away from each other, this may be indicative of a cause for concern.
- Unnecessary movement of monies and movement to alternative jurisdictions and into/out of high-risk jurisdictions.

Where a solicitor is concerned about possible money laundering activity, they must report their concerns.

The initial report should be made to the firm's nominated Money Laundering Reporting officer. It is then the role of the Reporting Officer to evaluate the information available with a view to deciding whether to make a suspicious activity report to the National Crime Agency.

If the Reporting Officer knows or suspects money laundering has taken place, then they must make a report as soon as is reasonably practicable and this should be prior to the completion of any transaction on behalf of the client.

Suspicious activity reports can be made by post or by fax, and there is a designated online system provided by the National Crime Agency.

Where a solicitor or a nominated officer fails to report a matter involving money laundering then they are likely to have committed an offence under the Proceeds of Crime Act 2002.

9.5 The Proceeds of Crime Act 2002

The Proceeds of Crime Act 2002 outlines the main offences of money laundering. It is a general piece of legislation that applies to everyone, but it is notable as it does contain a number of offences that are specific to those engaged in business within a regulated sector – such as solicitors.

9.5.1 Offences

The Act contains a number of offences that are characterised as either direct or non-direct offences.

Direct Offences

Direct offences are offences where the defendant is directly involved in the money laundering activity. For example, a solicitor transfers criminal property in contravention of the regulations.

Direct offences are as follows:

Section 327 – Concealing

A solicitor commits an offence if he takes steps to conceal, disguise, convert of transfer the proceeds of crime, or removes the proceeds of crime outside of UK jurisdiction.

Section 328 – Arranging

A solicitor commits an offence if he enters into or becomes concerned in an arrangement, which a person knows or suspects facilitates the retention, use or control of the proceeds of crime.

Section 329 – Acquisition

A solicitor commits an offence if he acquires, uses or possesses the proceeds of crime.

Non-Direct Offences

The non-direct offences that are part of the Proceeds of Crime Act 2002 are offences that can be committed by those in the regulated sector, and they involve a failure to respond appropriately to possible money laundering activity.

Non-direct offences are:

Section 330 – Failure to disclose

A solicitor commits an offence under the Act if they fail to disclose information about money laundering to the appropriate authorities.

Section 331 – Failure to disclose (nominated officers)

It is an offence on the part of a firm's nominated officer to fail to disclose information about money laundering activity to the appropriate authorities.

Section 333A – Tipping off

It is an offence for an individual to tip off another that an investigation into money laundering is underway.

Section 342 – Prejudicing

It is an offence for an individual to prejudice an investigation that is ongoing into money laundering activity.

Defences

Along with the direct and non-direct offences listed within the Proceeds of Crime Act 2002, it is important to note that a range of offence specific defences are available.

THE CONSENT DEFENCE

It is possible to present a defence to the offences of concealing (s327), arranging (s328) or acquiring (s329) based upon the defence of consent. The consent defence applies when a nominating officer submits a suspicious activity request to the National Crime Agency and requests consent to complete activities that would otherwise be prohibited.

REASONABLE EXCUSE

The defence of reasonable excuse applies when a nominated officer fails to make an authorised disclosure but has a reasonable excuse for failing to make the report as required under the regulations. It is important to note that there exists no statutory guidance as to what would be considered reasonable in this regard. This defence can apply to the offences of concealing (s327), arranging (s328) or acquiring (s329), failure to disclose (s330) and where a nominated officer fails to disclose (s331).

ADEQUATE CONSIDERATION

The adequate consideration defence only applies to section 329 – acquisition. The defence does not apply in circumstances where the solicitor has been paid disproportionately for the work completed and is similarly redundant where the solicitor knew or suspected that money laundering was in operation. However, it can be used in other circumstances where adequate payment has been received for the work completed.

TRAINING

It is of note that the money laundering regulations place a duty upon a legal practice to ensure that adequate training is provided to staff within the business. It is therefore a defence to offences under section 330 (failure to disclose) if a solicitor has not been provided the required training. This would only be the case in circumstances where actual knowledge or suspicion were absent.

PRIVILEGED CIRCUMSTANCES

A solicitor's duty of confidentiality, and the notion of legal privilege, can also provide a defence to a section 330 offence. The defence will not apply if the information given to the solicitor is such that it is clear that the transaction is linked to criminal activity.

LEGAL OVERSEAS CONDUCT

The final defence applies to both section 330 and section 331 offences. This states that where the criminal act took place in an alternative jurisdiction, in which the act was not illegal, and the act was such that it would be punishable with a sentence of less than 12 months' imprisonment, then the defence can be raised.

Chapter 9 Revision Points

Within this chapter we have considered a number of aspects of the SRA SQE1 syllabus on Legal Services. This includes consideration of the Equality Act including prohibited conduct and solicitor's obligations. We have also considered the key responsibilities that are placed upon the legal profession from the legislation regarding money laundering and the Proceeds of Crime Act.

It is important to check your knowledge using the following Multiple Choice Questions.

Multiple Choice Questions

Question 1

A recently graduated litigation assistant has started a new job. He works in a team of lawyers whereby he is the only male. He has been subjected to several sexual innuendos and has rejected a sexual approach from his line manager. Since the rejection, he has also noted that he is treated differently from the other members in his team. This ranges from not being allowed to leave early, having to do the lunch run on a daily basis (even though two other female litigation assistants started with him) and not being given a salary increase, despite the other two new starters getting one. The reason for this was because his work was not 'satisfactory,' despite his line manager not raising any objections and he is being congratulated on the quality of his work by his clients and recording more billable hours than the other two new starters.

He notes that no training has been provided by the firm, and when he queried this with the Senior Partner, the Senior Partner stated that the Litigation Assistant did not need to do that, as 'we're well versed in this area.' He assures him that he will speak with the team to ensure that everything is equal.

Nothing changes, so he leaves his job.

He is now considering submitting a claim to an Employment Tribunal.

Which of the following best describes the likely outcome of such a claim?

A. His line manager and the firm will be liable for harassment.
B. The firm is not liable for the line manager's behaviour because it did not know about how he was being treated.
C. His line manager's behaviour will not be considered unlawful because it was justified, as being in the lead for billing meant he had the time to do the lunch runs.
D. The litigation assistant will not be entitled to damages because they have not suffered any financial losses.
E. The firm alone will be liable for harassment.

Question 2

You have taken on a new instruction of the conveyance of a property and are meeting with the client in the afternoon. The client has been recommended to you by an old university acquaintance whom you trust.

In the meeting, while conducting due diligence, the client was unable to declare his passport, as it had very recently gone missing. He was awaiting a new one, but with time being of the essence, he was likely to lose his property purchase due to delays at the passport office. He did, however, have a credit card statement which confirmed his identity.

The client did state that he would have a look for his driving licence but was again unsure of its whereabouts. He returned later in the afternoon and was not in a position to present his driving licence but did have a letter from the old university acquaintance corroborating who he was.

The client thanked you for this, and as a favour, so the conveyance could be quickly completed, he would deposit the full amount in cash later on that day.

Which of the following best explains what the solicitor should do?

A. Commence the conveyance pending speaking to your acquaintance directly and asking him to sign and date the letter.
B. As he has come recommended, commence the conveyance. It's highly unlikely that there will be any issues regarding money laundering as he is a friend of your acquaintance.
C. Refuse to act because the client's identification verification has not been completed.
D. Proceed and complete the purchase because the letter is independent verification of the client's identity.
E. Proceed and complete the purchase because the credit card details contain his personal information.

Question 3

You have been instructed by your client, a footballer, in the purchase of shares in a global company listed on the London Stock Exchange. It has also come to your attention that the client has also instructed another department in your firm in relation to an ongoing investigation into his tax affairs in Spain, where he plays football professionally. You also recall reading something in the news about this. Complying with your duties, you make a disclosure to your firm's nominated officer, from whom you do not get a response, and no reports are filed to external bodies.

Not having heard anything, you execute the purchase of the shares for your client.

What is the likelihood that you have committed an offence under the Proceeds of Crime Act 2002?

A. Yes, because a suspicious activity report has not been made to the National Crime Agency.
B. No, because any criminal conduct took place outside the UK.
C. No, because the client has not yet been convicted of any criminal offence.
D. No, because the solicitor made an authorised disclosure to the firm's nominated officer.
E. Yes, because the solicitor did not have appropriate consent to proceed with the purchase of the shares.

10 Financial Services

10.1 SQE1 Syllabus

It may, on the surface, seem strange to think of financial services with regards to the work of those in the legal profession. However, it is important to note how a solicitor's professional code of conduct obligations require that we consider the often complicated and highly expert world of financial services.

The SQE1 syllabus requires an understanding of the regulatory framework, the concepts of specified investments, specified activities and exemptions and the overarching legislative framework provided by the Financial Services and Markets Act 2000.

10.2 Chapter Overview

It is important to note at the outset that the purpose of this chapter is not to make the reader expert in the field. However, it is important to ensure that there is an understanding of how the legal and financial worlds often meet and how these require the legal professional to consider how to act, based upon SRA Principle 7 – the duty to act in a client's best interests – and paragraph 3.2 of the SRA Code of Conduct that confirms that a solicitor must be competent to advise a client in the matter at hand.

So, how may a solicitor engage with the financial services world. There are a number of examples that may assist:

- If a solicitor acts for a client with regards to a successful claim for damages, in a matter involving a child, it is important that advice can be provided with regards to the investment of damages on behalf of the minor client.
- In probate, solicitors may be tasked with advising executors (or may be an executor themselves) and this may involve the sale of estate assets.
- In conveyancing, it is highly likely that a client will need a mortgage, or other financial support arranged such as a life insurance policy.
- In the corporate side of legal practice, a solicitor may be advising or assisting in the purchase of company shares or equities or arranging finance for an acquisition.

DOI: 10.4324/9781003435525-17

- In family law work, an understanding of finance and assets is often required and may involve assisting clients to consider the reinvestment of funds granted as part of the divorce or separation process.

It is easy to see the challenges that can be faced by a solicitor in simply demonstrating the level of expertise required to meet their code of conduct obligations. However, there are even more stringent measures that must be considered as solicitors who engage in any element of financial advice are subject to the same legislation as those who operate within the financial sector on a day-to-day basis. The relevant legislation being the Financial Services and Markets Act 2000 and the wide range of statutory instruments and rules that support the Act.

10.3 Financial Services Regulatory Structure

There are two main bodies who regulate the area of financial services. These are the Financial Conduct Authority and the Prudential Regulation Authority. These were created under the Financial Services Act 2012. In addition, the overall monitoring of the UK financial system is the responsibility of the Financial Policy Committee. We shall consider each of these in turn.

10.3.1 The Financial Conduct Authority

Within the Financial Services and Markets Act 2000, the Financial Conduct Authority is set a range of objectives, these are:

- Consumer protection.
- Protecting the integrity of the UK financial system.
- Promoting effective competition.

In carrying out these objectives the Authority has overall responsibility for monitoring the conduct of regulated standard firms and also the regulation of all prudential regulated firms that are not regulated directly by the Prudential Regulation Authority.

To complete this task the Financial Conduct Authority is given a range of powers that can require firms to withdraw or amend misleading offers, that can block the introduction of new services, or can even require firms to stop a particular product.

Despite the wide-ranging remit and powers held by the Financial Conduct Authority, it is likely that consumers will only typically be aware of the Authority due to their role in the regulation of consumer credit and second charge mortgages.

10.3.2 The Prudential Regulation Authority

The Financial Services and Markets Act 2000 identifies that firms that will fall under the auspices of the Prudential Regulation Authority will be those that undertake any of a range of prescribed financial activities including accepting deposits, managing contracts of insurance or dealing with investments.

The Prudential Regulation Authority therefore regulates and supervises the operation of banks, building societies, insurers, some investment firms, Lloyds of London and credit unions.

10.4 The Financial Services and Markets Act 2000 and the Legal Profession

The Financial Service and Markets Act 2000 sets out the requirement that any business that carries out 'regulated activities' must be authorised by the appropriate regulator. Of course, legal practices are regulated already via the Solicitors Regulation Authority and therefore it could be the case that firms may need two forms of regulation to be in operation simultaneously.

To avoid the possibility of overregulation, the Act contains special provisions that relate to professional firms such as legal practices. The Act confirms that where financial operations are aligned to the standard operation of the professional firm, then, subject to certain conditions, the firm will be exempt from having to be regulated by the Financial Conduct Authority. In these circumstances the SRA will retain sole regulatory responsibility over the legal practice.

Even where this measure does assist it is important to note that there are two main restrictions that are placed upon legal practices. The first is found within section 19 of the Financial Services and Markets Act 2000 and is referred to as 'the general prohibition.' The second is outlined under section 21 of the Act and is known as the 'financial promotion prohibition.'

10.4.1 The General Prohibition

Under section 19 of the Act, it is confirmed that:

> No person may carry on a regulated activity in the UK unless authorised or exempt.

The Act further confirms that an authorised person is someone who has been granted permission by the appropriate regulator. Should an individual carry out a regulated activity without the permission required then, under section 23 of the Financial Services and Markets Act 2000, they may be found guilty of a criminal offence that could be punishable by up to two years imprisonment or by an unlimited fine.

Consideration of regulated activities will be given in section 10.5.

10.4.2 The Financial Promotion Prohibition

Similarly, under section 21 of the Act, an unauthorised person would commit a criminal offence if they were to offer a financial promotion without having the required authorisation to do so.

10.5 Regulated Activities

Section 22 of the Financial Services and Markets Act 2000 states that:

1) An activity is a regulated activity for the purposes of this Act if it is an activity of a specified kind which is carried on by way of business and –
   a. relates to an investment of a specified kind; or
   b. in the case of an activity of a kind which is also specified for the purposes of this paragraph, is carried on in relation to property of any kind.
2) An activity is also a regulated activity for the purposes of this Act if it is an activity of a specified kind which is carried on by way of business and relates to –
   a. information about a person's financial standing.
3) An activity is also a regulated activity for the purposes of this Act if it is an activity of a specified kind which –
   a. is carried on by way of business in Great Britain, and
   b. is, or relates to, claims management services.

Looking specifically at subsection 1 – it is clear that a number of tests must be considered in assessing whether a matter is one that would be described as regulated activity.

10.5.1 The Four Tests

The four tests to consider are as follows:

- Are you in business?
- Does the transaction feature:
  a. a specified investment;
  b. information about a person's financial standing; or
  c. the setting of a specified benchmark?
- Is there a specified activity?
- Does an exclusion apply?

10.5.2 Are You in Business?

If the activity is to be considered regulated it must be carried out in the course of business. Whilst it is noted that the concept of a business could be the subject of considerable debate, the question in most circumstances should be considered in plain and simple terms. So, if a solicitor were giving advice in a live file within the legal practice, then that would clearly be undertaken within the business.

10.5.3 Specified Investments

Specified investments are defined under Schedule 2 of FSMA and in the Financial Services and Markets Act 2000 (Regulated Activities) Order 2001, often referred to as the RAO.

Under the RAO, a number of types of investments are outlined that meet the specified investment criteria, these are:

- Shares in a company.
- Instruments creating or acknowledging indebtedness (e.g. debentures, debenture stock, loan stock, bonds and so on).
- Government and public securities (including UK government gilts).
- Certain instruments giving entitlement to an investment (e.g. warrants).
- Regulated collective investment schemes (e.g. unit trusts, investment companies, open-ended investment companies).
- Various derivatives including options, futures and contracts for difference (CFDs).
- Rights under a contract of insurance, including life assurance policies and 'general insurance' policies such as defective title, buildings and contents insurance.
- Lloyd's syndicate capacity and syndicate membership.
- Deposits (which would include money in a bank account).
- Rights under a regulated mortgage contract (RMC), home reversion plan, home purchase plan or sale and rent-back mortgages.
- Rights under a stakeholder or personal pension scheme (but not employer/occupational pensions).
- ISAs, if the vehicle contains one of these investments.

It should be noted that products of the National Savings and Investment Bank, such as Premium Bonds and National Savings Certificates, are not specified investments.

Other common investments such as land, wine, stamps, art and vintage cars are also not specified investments for the purposes of the Act.

10.5.4 Is There a Specified Activity?

The specified activities and specified investments are defined in Schedule 2 of FSMA and in the Financial Services and Markets Act 2000 (Regulated Activities) Order 2001 (the RAO).

The main activities relevant to a solicitor are:

a) Dealing as an agent – RAO Article 21 – would involve a solicitor buying, selling, subscribing for or underwriting investments on behalf of a client. The key consideration being that the role of the solicitor commits that client to transactions.

b) Arranging – RAO Article 25 – In transactions that involve the purchase of insurance – such as a life insurance policy as part of a conveyancing process – or the purchase of investments – such as equities or shares as an aspect of administration of probate, it is often the case that a solicitor will liaise with the client on one side and an intermediary such as an insurance company or a stockbroker on the other. It is in these circumstances that the solicitor may be considered to be arranging.
c) Managing – RAO Article 37 – is a stage beyond the process of arranging and involves the solicitor taking an active role via a discretionary power granted by the client. This is a common occurrence where a solicitor is involved in the administration of probate as a trustee, executor or administrator.
d) Safeguarding – RAO Article 40 – The activity consisting of both the safeguarding of assets belonging to another, and the administration of those assets or arranging for one or more other persons to carry on that activity. Again, this is a common occurrence when dealing with probate and trust work.
e) Advising – RAO Article 53 – This involves the giving of advice on the merits of buying, selling, subscribing for or underwriting an investment. This article requires that the advice given is specific and not general in nature to trigger the regulated activity element.

10.5.5 Exclusions

Exclusions under Schedule 2 of FSMA and in the Financial Services and Markets Act 2000 (Regulated Activities) Order 2001 (the RAO) are available. These exclusions have the effect of removing otherwise regulated activity from consideration under the regulations.

This change may result in a solicitor not requiring authorisation.

There is a range of exclusions available with the most relevant to solicitors being:

a) Introducing – This exclusion is specifically tied to the activity of arranging – outlined earlier. For the exclusion to apply the circumstances of the transaction must be such that the solicitor has simply taken the step of introducing the client to an authorised person and nothing further.
b) Using an Authorised Third Person – This exclusion is available to activities that would be considered under the activity of dealing as an agent and the activity of arranging. The Authorised Third Person term refers to a person who is authorised by the FCA. The process is one where the transaction is entered into based upon the advice of the Authorised Third Person and not on any guidance provided by the solicitor.
c) The execution-only client exclusion – This exclusion is available to activities that involve dealing as an agent and also arranging. The execution-only exemption operates in a similar fashion as the Authorised Third Person

approach but simply removes the requirement for an authorised person's involvement. Instead, the exemption can be relied upon in circumstances where the client has not sought advice from the solicitor regarding the transaction.

d) The trustee or personal representative exemption – This exclusion has a much wider remit and can be used with regards to matters of arranging, managing, safeguarding and the advising of fellow trustees and/or beneficiaries. It should be noted that as well as matters that relate to probate and estate administration the exemption is also used with regards to lending money on or administering regulated mortgage contracts.
   The exemption also features specific limitations which are as follows:
   - The exemption is available if a solicitor acts as a trustee, executor or administrator but does not apply in circumstances where they are working for a trustee, executor or administrator.
   - The exemption also applied if the solicitor is a trustee, executor or administrator but the specified activity is actually carried out by someone else within the legal practice.
   - The exclusion cannot be used in circumstances where the solicitor has been renumerated specifically for providing the specified activity.
   - The exemption cannot be used in relation to matters that involve contracts of insurance or the pursuance of an insurance distribution.

e) The professional/necessary exclusion
   - This exemption can be used with regards to matters that involve arranging, safeguarding and dealing as an agent with the exclusion applying where the activity is required to be performed as a necessary aspect of the other services that are being provided by the solicitor to the client. Once again, the exclusion cannot be relied upon in circumstances where the solicitor is involved in pursuing an insurance distribution on behalf of the client or being renumerated separately for the specified activity.

f) The takeover exclusion
   - The exclusion applies in the following circumstances:
   - the transaction is one to acquire or dispose of shares in a body corporate (other than an open-ended investment company) or which is entered into for the purposes of such an acquisition or disposal; and
   - either:
     I. the conditions set out in the paragraph below are met, or
     II. those conditions are not met, but the object of the transaction may nevertheless reasonably be regarded as being the acquisition of day-to-day control of the affairs of the body corporate.

The (b)(i) exclusion covers the highly specific situation where control in the body corporate is passing from a specified group to another group.

Exclusion (b)(ii) applies a more generic exemption as this only requires that a group of persons is acting together for the test to be met. In addition, the legal practice must be advising the party, or multiple parties, that are seeking to acquire day-to-day control. It is important to note that the exemption does not require that the firm is advising all the shareholders, but they must be advising the controlling group.

It is important to note that paragraph (b)(i) requires specified conditions to be met, these are:

a) the shares consist of or include 50 per cent or more of the voting shares in the body corporate; or
b) the shares, together with any already held by the person acquiring them, consist of or include at least 50 per cent of such shares, and
c) in either case, the vendor and acquirer are: a body corporate; a partnership; a single individual; or a group of connected individuals. It is not necessary for the vendor and the acquirer to be the same 'type.'

The effect of condition (b) is to make the exclusion available for transactions where a small shareholding is changing hands, but the acquirer has, or will have after the transaction, control of the body corporate.

Condition (c) must be met by both acquirer and vendor, even though the firm may only be advising one of the respective parties. It should be noted that both the acquirer and vendor do not have to be the same type of entity, but each must fall into just one type.

Finally, a group of connected individuals is defined as:

a) In relation to the vendor, a single group of persons, each of whom is:
    i. a director or manager of the body corporate;
    ii. a close relative of any such director or manager, or
    iii. a person acting as trustee for any person falling within paragraphs (i) or (ii).
b) In relation to the acquirer, a single group of persons, each of whom is:
    i. a person who is or is to be a director or manager of the body corporate;
    ii. a close relative of any such person, or
    iii. a person acting as trustee for any person falling within paragraphs (i) or (ii).

10.6 Professional Body Exemption

Of significant importance to solicitors is the exemption for professional firms that is outlined in section 327 of the Act. The significance of the exemption to legal practitioners can be simply viewed as a means that allows those who are already regulated by the SRA to not have to also be regulated by another designated body such as the Financial Conduct Authority.

Section 327 of the Act (Exemption from the general prohibition) sets out the conditions which must be met for a person to be treated as an exempt professional firm, and for the person's regulated activities to be treated as exempt regulated activities.

The conditions are as follows:

1) The person seeking to use the exemption must be –
   a. a member of a profession; or
   b. controlled or managed by one or more such members.
2) The person must not receive from a person other than his client any pecuniary reward or other advantage, for which he does not account to his client, arising out of his carrying on of any of the activities.
3) The manner of the provision by the person of any service in the course of carrying on the activities must be incidental to the provision by him of professional services.
4) The Person must not carry on, or hold himself out as carrying on, a regulated activity other than –
   a. one which rules made as a result of section 332(3) allow him to carry on; or
   b. one in relation to which he is an exempt person.
5) The activities must not be of a description, or relate to an investment of a description, specified in an order made by the Treasury for the purposes of this subsection.
6) The activities must be the only regulated activities carried on by the person (other than regulated activities in relation to which he is an exempt person).

10.7 SRA Financial Services (Conduct of Business Rules)

As outlined earlier, the SRA, through the Law Society of England and Wales, is considered to be a designated professional body under Part 20 of the Financial Services and Markets Act. This ensures that firms that are regulated by the SRA may engage in financial services activities without requiring specific regulation by the Financial Conduct Authority subject to the section 327 conditions discussed previously.

To assist individual solicitors and legal practices with this tricky area of regulatory practice, the SRA set out the scope of regulated financial activities that may be undertaken within the SRA Financial Services (Scope) Rules 2018.

The rules are a means to regulate the approach that firms take to financial services provision under the professional exemption.

Rules 2.1 and 2.2 – Status Disclosure

A firm must provide to the client correct information about the regulatory status of the firm. This information must be provided to the client in a manner that is clear, fair and does not mislead.

Rule 3.1 – Best Execution

Echoing SRA Principle 7, a solicitor must apply the duty of working in the best interests of the client. It is therefore important to ensure that matters are progressed expeditiously unless it is clearly not in the best interest of the client to do so.

Rules 4.1 and 4.2 – Transactions

A legal practice is required to make, maintain and store records of both client instructions to carry out transactions and instructions that are provided to third parties to action client requests.

Rule 5.1 – Commissions

The legal practice is also required to ensure that records are made, maintained and stored of any and all commissions received in relation to regulated activities and how the firm ensured that the payment was correctly ascribed.

Rule 7.1 – Execution-Only Clients

As discussed previously in the chapter, there are specific actions required in matters that relate to execution only – where no advice is provided. In these matters, Rule 7.1 requires that confirmation is provided in writing that confirms that the client is not relying upon the advice of the solicitor. A copy of the correspondence would then be attached to the client file.

COB Rules, Part 3 – Insurance Distribution Activities

In matters that relate to insurance distribution activities, it is important to note that adequate communication is required with the client. This requires that the legal professional is again providing clear, fair and non-misleading information to the client. In addition, the solicitor must also ensure that the client is provided with a breakdown of renumeration received in relation to any contract of insurance and this must be provided before the matter is concluded.

Chapter 10 Revision Points

Within this chapter we have considered a number of aspects of the SRA SQE1 syllabus on Legal Services. This includes consideration of the Financial Regulations that underpin the work of the legal practice. Consideration was given to the regulatory structure, regulated activity and the exclusions that assist legal professionals.

It is important to check your knowledge using the following Multiple Choice Questions.

Multiple Choice Questions

Question 1

A legal practice acts for a longstanding client who is a shareholder and director of Widgets Ltd. During a client meeting it is stated that the client does not wish to continue as a director of the company due to ill-health and therefore wishes to retire. The solicitor asks about the shareholding, and it is confirmed that the client has been able to arrange for the sale of all shares to a fellow director. The shares amount to 75% of the share capital. The client instructs the solicitor that he requires advice on the sale of the shares. The solicitor is also required to prepare the contractual documentation and may be required to negotiate terms on behalf of the client. The legal practice is not authorised by the Financial Conduct Authority to carry out regulated activities under the Financial Services and Markets Act 2000.

Which of the following options enables the solicitor to advise and act as the client requests?

A. The solicitor can act as shares in private companies are not specified investments.
B. The solicitor can rely on the 'takeover' exclusion.
C. The solicitor can rely on the exemption for professional firms.
D. The solicitor would be exempt as they would only be giving generic advice.
E. The solicitor can act as they would not be carrying out a specified investment activity.

Question 2

You have just settled a matter for a client whereby your client is seeking advice on whether the damages received can be spent on a buy to let property. You are not familiar with the property market, and it is not an area that you work in. That said, the client wishes for you to provide your thoughts and advice. You are aware that your firm is not authorised by the FCA to undertake any activities under the Financial Services and Markets Act 2000.

Which of the following would apply should you provide advice to your client?

A. You will have complied with your obligations to act in the best interest of your client.
B. Criminal proceedings may be initiated against the firm, but not you personally.
C. Disciplinary action may be taken against you.
D. You have complied with the rules of integrity and honesty by providing an answer to your client's query.
E. Criminal proceedings may be initiated against you.

Question 3

You have settled a case for a client whereby he has been awarded £1.7 million in damages. Your client has asked about investing some of the compensation into crypto assets. You refer the client to an independent advisor who specialises in crypto-assets and following the meeting, the client asks you to purchase crypto-assets for him. As a means of gratitude, he allocates 1 crypto coin to you, which is worth £11,400.00, which you have decided to keep.

Do your actions amount to a regulated activity under the Financial Services and Markets Act 2000?

A. No, because the exemptions allow for law firms to not be regulated.
B. Yes, because the solicitor received a pecuniary reward.
C. No, because crypto assets are not deemed to be specified investments under the Financial Services and Markets Act 2000.
D. Yes, because you lacked the necessary competence to complete this transaction.
E. No, because you advised the client to take advice from a third party.

11 Funding Legal Services

11.1 SQE1 Syllabus

The SQE1 syllabus requires an awareness of a range of options for the funding of legal services. These include private retainers, conditional fee arrangements, damages-based agreements, fixed fees, legal aid, third party funding and the use of legal expenses cover.

11.2 Chapter Overview

Within this chapter we will analyse the various pathways that are open to a client when legal actions are within contemplation.

11.3 Introduction

Any consideration of bringing legal action is one that necessarily requires the individual client to consider how the matter will be funded. Consideration must be given to how you will fund your own legal costs, but consideration must also be given to ongoing costs such as court fees and expert witness report costs. It should also be noted that the legal system in England and Wales requires parties to think about how the other side's costs will be met, should an adverse result occur.

Post the Legal Aid, Sentencing and Punishment or Offenders Act 2012, many aspects of public funding for legal cases have been subject to severe restrictions and it has often fallen to legal practices to find approaches to funding that allow those with legal matters to seek a fair resolution. This requires consideration of fixed fees, conditional fee arrangements, damages-based agreements and the legal aid options that are still available.

11.4 Funding Options

11.4.1 Privately Funded Matters

The simplest form of funding available to a client is to simply fund their own legal action via their own means. This can be an option that is selected specifically due

DOI: 10.4324/9781003435525-18

to the nature of the matter or circumstances that are specific to the individual. It may also be the case that the matter is such that there exists no alternative option for funding of the legal issue at hand.

Privately funded matters require a calculation to be completed of the costs of the case. These costs will include a number of components with the primary consideration being one of the legal professional's time. There exists a guideline set of rates for solicitors that is provided via the gov.uk website, and it is a simple case of multiplying the number of hours spent on a matter by the solicitor's hourly rate to arrive at the initial component of legal costs.

In addition, to the direct solicitor cost, there are also disbursements and expenses that need to be considered as well. These are charged separately but are clearly a consideration for the client.

Within the private funding model, one of the greatest challenges is the open-ended nature of fees. Although clients will be informed at the start of the matter which level of fee earner will be working on their case and the hourly rates of that person, the total cost will not be possible to confirm as this will entirely depend on a multitude of case specific factors.

The role of the legal professional, at the outset of a private funding arrangement, is to ensure that the best possible information is given with a view to allowing the client to assess the likely total costs of taking legal action, as ultimately, the costs are the responsibility of the client.

11.4.2 Fixed Fees

Privately funded matters require clients to make decisions about risk and reward at the outset that may well lead to the conclusion of not wishing to take a matter forward. There has therefore been a movement towards fixed fee arrangements as a means to providing assurance to clients at the outset and therefore help the legal practice to build their client numbers.

Fixed fees, as the name suggests, involve the solicitor completing the direct solicitor cost component of the process at a fixed and agreed fee, although it should be noted that this would still involve the addition of VAT and the payment of disbursements as additional sums to consider.

Due to the certainty over the fee these types of arrangement have proven popular for many years in areas of legal work such as conveyancing transactions. However, the move away from legal aid funding has resulted in a move towards fixed fee cases in areas such as private client work or family law cases.

It should also be noted that the removal of legal aid has also led to the rise of the litigant in person, a situation where the client chooses to pursue a matter without instructing formal legal representation. In turn this has led to a sub-level of fixed fee work for solicitors as litigants in person instruct a solicitor but only for specific aspects of the case, such as drafting proceedings, or attendance at a hearing.

Whilst fixed fees allow greater client assurance, they are a significant balancing act for legal professionals. It is important to ensure that fixed fee levels are in line with the actual expectations that will be placed upon the solicitor during the case. It is all well and good having case work but too many unprofitable cases can question the viability of the legal venture.

For the same reason, it is important that fixed fee advertisements are clear on what is, and what is not, included for the fee quoted.

11.4.3 Conditional Fee Agreements (CFA)

Conditional fee agreements, often referred to as 'no win, no fee' agreements are defined formally within section 58(2(a) of the Courts and Legal Services Act 1990 as:

> An agreement with a person providing advocacy or litigation services which provides for his fees and expenses, or any part of them, to be payable only in specified circumstances.

As denoted by the 'no win, no fee' tag that is often applied to CFA's, the specified circumstances mentioned within the definition relate to whether the client succeeds as either claimant or defendant in the case.

CFA's again feature a balance between risk and reward for the legal professional. There is a substantial risk aligned with taking on a matter that may be unsuccessful, as the solicitor completes all of the work and may receive a nominal or even no payment for their endeavours should the case be lost. Alternatively, a solicitor may receive enhanced renumeration in the event of a successful case outcome.

As the provisions of a CFA commit the client and the solicitor to these positions it is essential that the agreement complies with the formal requirements outlined in section 58 and 58A of the Courts and Legal Services Act 1990. These requirements are:

a) The CFA must relate to a matter of civil litigation excluding family law matters.
b) The CFA must be in writing and evidenced as such within the legal file.
c) The CFA must be clear, fair and unambiguous with regards to the fees that would be payable under the agreement if successful or unsuccessful.

This final point is key when consideration is given of success fees. Success fee is the typical name given to the uplift amount that will be payable on a successful case. This is typically expressed in terms of a percentage and can be as high as 100% of the solicitor's normal charges.

So should a solicitor take on a high-risk matter, they may apply a higher success fee to recognise the additional risk of the legal matter. If the solicitor would normally charge £200 per hour, they would actually be entitled to double this sum if a successful outcome is achieved.

In personal injury claims, there is an additional cap of 25% of general damages recovered.

The whole area of CFA's also needs to be considered in light of the system within English law of 'loser pays.' It should be noted that a successful case outcome may lead to an order that the winner's costs are paid by the opponent. Where this happens, it should be noted that the success fee element would still remain the responsibility of the client.

The game of risk/reward is therefore being played by both the client and the legal professional.

To assist the legal professional to minimise the risks of taking a case forward, a process of risk assessment is typically used. The risk assessment process would involve an assessment of:

- The likely success of the case.
- The likely amount of damages that would be recoverable.
- The likely timeframe between engagement and resolution.
- The amount of time that the solicitor is likely to be required to employ in taking the matter through from instruction to a possible future trial.

The risk assessment therefore advises the solicitor on the viability of the case but also allows for a reasoned approach to be taken to the level of any success fee that will be applied to the case.

11.4.4 Damages-Based Agreements (DBA)

Damages-based agreements are a contingency fee arrangement that requires the claimant, on the completion of a set event (usually a successful outcome in the case) to then pay the solicitor for the work completed.

DBAs are defined by section 58AA(3)(a) of the Court's and Legal Services Act 1990 as:

> An agreement between a person providing advocacy services, litigation services or claims management services and the recipient of those services which provides that –
>
> I. the recipient is to make a payment to the person providing the services if the recipient obtains a specified financial benefit in connection with the matter in relation to which the services are provided, and
>
> II. the amount of that payment is to be determined by reference to the amount of the financial benefit obtained.

The use of a DBA is another example of both client and solicitor having to assess risks in a similar way to with a CFA.

Under a DBA, the client commits at the outset to pay an agreed percentage of the compensation received to the solicitor for the work that has been completed. This is an approach which is founded in the notion of access to justice as there is no payment required except where a successful outcome is achieved, and this would only be at the very end of the case. However, if an agreement is put in place that sets the agreed fee as 10% of damages recovered and the case then resolves for £200,000, then the client is bound to pay the solicitor the sum of £20,000, regardless of the amount of time, work or effort that has been required to achieve case resolution.

DBA's, due to the specific link to damages paid, tend to only be available for claimants.

To be enforceable, the DBA must be compliant with the requirements of section 58AA(4) Courts and Legal Services Act 1990 and the Damages-Based Agreements Regulations 2013 (SI 2013/609). These state that the DBA must:

- Be in writing.
- Specify the specific proceedings to which the agreement relates.
- Clearly and unambiguously specify the circumstances under which the fee will be payable.
- Include a rationale for the level of fee that is to be charged.

Regarding this final point, it is important to note that limits are placed upon the level of any DBA fee with a maximum cap of 50% of general damages. This is reduced to a lower 25% cap for personal injury cases and a maximum of 35% applies for employment matters.

11.4.5 Legal Expenses Insurance

Legal expenses is an alternative way of funding legal action. Insurance products can be used as a means to fund all or part of a legal action and can even assist with the funding of additional costs such as disbursements or adverse costs.

Broadly speaking there are two forms of legal expenses insurance – Before the Event Insurance and After the Event Insurance.

Before the Event Insurance

Before the Event Insurance is a form of insurance against possible future legal costs – hence the phrase 'before the event.'

Often Before the Event Insurance is purchased alongside other insurance products such as household or car insurance, rather than on a standalone basis.

The policy provides the individual with a means of funding legal advice, legal representation and/or legal services. It should be noted that the scope and coverage will vary with each individual policy.

In theory the use of the insurance policy should ensure that where a claim is accepted, the insurer will then be liable to pay the solicitor's fees as well as any incidental costs incurred in the legal process.

In reality the policies tend to be tied to the specific provider and will often require the case to be passed to a member of that firm's panel, rather than allowing the client to choose who they wish to represent them. It should also be noted that it is common for the policy to feature a cap on the amount of legal expenses that can be covered with the client then potentially liable for any shortfall.

It is noted that further to the case of *Sarwar v Alam* [2001] EWCA Civ 1401, it is accepted practice that a solicitor should seek to establish the existence of any legal expenses insurance at the outset of the case and should seek to advise the client accordingly.

After the Event Insurance

After the Event Insurance is a specific type of insurance product that is taken out after a legal dispute has arisen. The policy is often specifically advised for clients as a means to provide cover in most civil cases with regards to the legal expenses incurred in making or defending a case.

It is common in practice for an After the Event Insurance policy to be taken out as part of arrangements under either a damages-based agreement or conditional fee agreement.

After the Event Insurance policies are charged on a risk analysis basis with policies taken out earlier in a case often costing less than policies taken out when the matter is approaching a court date. Further factors in the price include the chance of success and the level of costs that require cover.

11.4.6 Third Party Funding

As the name suggests, third party funding refers to cases where a third party, unconnected to the proceedings, agrees to fund the costs of litigation.

Third party funding can take many forms including philanthropy, support for a cause or crowd funding. However, the most common form of third party funding is tied to commercial funders who seek to realise a profitable return in return for their agreement to fund the client's costs and disbursements.

Historically, the use of commercial funding was viewed as unlawful or immoral as it raised concerns regarding third party control in proceedings and this was viewed as a potential barrier to the correct administration of justice. However, further to the case of *Arkin v Borchard Lines Ltd* [2005] EWCA Civ 655, it is noted that the court's view has changed and third party funding is now viewed as a means to facilitate access to justice.

It is vital that any solicitor who is taking forward a claim in which third party funding operates must be aware of the need to ensure compliance with their own professional conduct responsibilities. This is particularly important in demonstrating conduct areas such as acting in the best interests of the client and conflicts of interest.

11.4.7 Legal Aid Funding

Legal aid is a means by which legal fees in both civil and criminal cases can be paid from public funds, should the client meet the required eligibility criteria.

The relevant legislation for this is provided through the Legal Aid, Sentencing and Punishment of Offenders Act 2012, and this is supported via a number of statutory instruments.

Civil Legal Aid

Historically, civil legal aid was available to those who had a meritorious case but lacked the financial means to be able to pursue a legal action. However, the introduction of the Legal Aid, Sentencing and Punishment of Offenders Act 2012 greatly reduced an individual's ability to use public funds to support a legal action. At the time of writing, civil legal aid is now only available in limited circumstances.

There are three general criteria that a client must now meet for them to be eligible to receive civil legal aid – scope, merit and means.

SCOPE

Whilst in the past, a wide range of matters including private family matters, employment law, immigration and clinical negligence fell within the requirements of legal aid, it is noted that post the Legal Aid, Sentencing and Punishment of Offenders Act 2012 these areas would now typically be considered to be out of scope.

In scope matters are typically restricted and include private family matters that involve domestic violence, matters that involve children, public family law proceedings such as care proceedings, matters centred on discrimination and cases where the individual is at substantial risk of homelessness.

Whilst this list is clearly highly restricted with regards to what can be funded it should be noted section 10 of the Act does allow any matter to be considered for funding under exceptional cases funding, but this is used in very limited circumstances.

For most cases, the next step would now be to move forward to consider both the merits and means tests. However, it is important to note that matters that involve parents or children involved in care proceedings do not need to consider the further tests.

MERITS

If the matter is within scope, the next step is to consider whether the case has sufficient merit to be publicly funded. An assessment of case merits requires the solicitor to assess the client's case with reference to the Civil Legal Aid (Merits Criteria) Regulations 2013 and the subsequent amendments to those regulations. Based upon these, consideration should be given to:

- Prospects of success.
- Proportionality.
- Is the case a matter of significant public interest?
- Could funding be secured via alternative means?
- The likely level of damages that could be awarded.
- Whether the case is of fundamental importance to the client.

MEANS

The final stage in the process requires consideration of whether the client is financially eligible to receive legal aid. This is calculated by reference to the individual's income and also the value of any assets that the person may hold. It should also be noted that consideration may also be given to the income or assets of the client's partner.

Where the client is in receipt of a relevant welfare benefit, they will automatically qualify for legal aid funding. Where this is not the case then a client will only be eligible where the total of their capital and income is below £8000 (£3000 in immigration cases).

Further tests require that a client's gross monthly income is calculated with values above £2657 ensuring that the client does not qualify for legal aid. For values below £2657, the final stage is to calculate the client's disposable income. This is calculated by deducting the client's living costs from their monthly income and only clients who has less than £733 per month of disposable income will qualify for legal aid.

Criminal Legal Aid

The rules determining whether an individual is eligible for criminal legal aid funding are contained within both the Legal Aid, Sentencing and Punishment of Offenders Act 2012 and within the Criminal Legal Aid (General) Regulations 2013.

The rules confirm that criminal legal aid is available to cover the cost of a defendant's legal representation should the eligibility criteria be satisfied.

To determine whether a client is eligible for criminal legal aid, consideration needs to be given as to the merits of the matter and the client's financial means.

MERITS

The merit test for criminal legal aid is often referred to as the 'interests of justice' test.

Under section 17(2) of the Legal Aid, Sentencing and Punishment of Offenders Act 2012, a series of tests are outlined to allow for a client's circumstances to be reviewed. These are as follows:

- Is the matter such that the client is likely to lose their liberty or their livelihood or suffer serious reputational damage?
- Is the matter such that the proceedings involve a substantial question of law?
- Is the client able to understand the court proceedings and to state their own case before the court?
- For the correct administration of justice, will the matter require the tracing, interviewing or the cross examination of expert witnesses?
- Would client representation be important to another person such as a vulnerable witness who may be subject to cross examination?
- Can the defendant demonstrate another relevant reason to show that the interests of justice will be served by granting legal aid?

If the case is committed, sent or transferred to the Crown Court then the interests of justice tests are considered to be automatically met.

MEANS

Clients are usually required to disclose full details of their financial circumstances prior to any confirmation of legal aid. The initial test that is used involves the calculation of a client's adjusted income. This is calculated via an analysis of the client's personal financial circumstances from which a deduction is made that takes into account the client's essential expenses. This provides a figure representing the client's disposable income. The figure decides whether all legal work is funded by the public purses, or whether the client is required to contribute to the legal fees.

Chapter 11 Revision Points

Within this chapter we have considered a number of aspects of the SRA SQE1 syllabus on Legal Services. This includes consideration of the funding options available for clients seeking to pursue legal matters. The chapter analysed public and privately funded options as well as the legal funding framework provided via CFA's and DBA arrangements.

It is important to check your knowledge using the following Multiple Choice Questions.

Multiple Choice Questions

Question 1

You are acting on behalf of a client who has the benefit of a 'CFA,' and a success fee of 25% in place.

Which of the following describes the position in relation to legal costs?

A. If the client wins, your fee will be calculated at 25% of the damages received.
B. If the client loses, the client will have to pay disbursements.
C. If the client wins, the opponent will pay the success fee.
D. If the client loses, your fee will be calculated at their usual charging rate.
E. If the client wins, the client will pay nothing in respect of their own costs.

Question 2

You have been asked by an acquaintance to take on a matter under the benefit of a DBA. Your initial assessment of the matter points to a successful claim. However, you are aware that a DBA is against firm policy. You have attempted to clarify this with your supervisor but have not yet received a response, and the client is pushing you.

Considering the rules under the SRA Principles, what should you do?

A. Agree, because you are acting in the client's best interests.
B. Refuse, because that is the firm's policy.
C. Agree, because the client is the instructor, and they decide how they wish to fund their claim.
D. Refuse, because there are alternative funding provisions that you can apply.
E. Agree, because your assessment shows that the claim will be successful.

Question 3

You have been instructed by your client who is subject to care proceedings from the local authority, as they are seeking an order to remove his children from his care.

Your client is in receipt of social welfare benefits and is on a low income with no savings. Upon your assessment of the matter, you are confident that your client can be successful, owing to a robust defence.

What is the likelihood that your client would be eligible to secure legal aid funding?

A. No, because as a defendant, he is not entitled to legal aid.
B. Yes, because the client satisfies both the means and the merits test.
C. No, because a client funding the matter privately would not fund this case, owing to the fact that a local authority would normally win.
D. Yes, because a client on a low income and social welfare benefits will qualify for legal aid.
E. No, because the subject matter of this case is not within the parameters (scope) of legal aid.

12 Answers to Multiple Choice Questions

12.1 Chapter Overview

This chapter provides the answers to the multiple choice questions at the end of each chapter of the book.

DOI: 10.4324/9781003435525-19

12.2 Chapter 1 – The Legal System of England and Wales

Question 1

Answer

Option C is correct. There were no trade unions prior to the 1800s, and the judiciary, the monarchy and the nobility played a significant role in the development of the legal system.

Question 2

Answer

Option E is correct. The application of the rule of law involves several key principles. Firstly, laws must be applied equally to all individuals, regardless of their status or position. This means that no one can be given special treatment or be exempt from the law. Secondly, laws must be enforced by an independent judiciary, free from political interference. Judges must interpret and apply the law impartially and without bias.

Question 3

Answer

Option B is correct. 'The King hath no prerogative, save that which the law of the land allows him.' This implied that the King (and as we know that the Royal Prerogative is exercised by ministers also) could not alter any aspect of common law without the consent of Parliament, nor could he declare an offence that had not previously existed.

12.3 Chapter 2 – Primary Legislation

Question 1

Answer

Option C is correct. Conventionally, we know that Royal Assent will be granted, but the final stage is that of Royal Assent.

Question 2

Answer

Option A is correct. The rule of implied repeal allows Parliament to change legislation by creating statutes that conflict with previous ones. In this case, this will be enough to render the (fictional) Acquisition of Land Act 2000 as repealed. However, do note our discussion in 2.3.3, where constitutional statutes are required to be expressely repealed in order to be valid.

Question 3

Answer

Option E is correct. As your local MP has been voted in via elective process, they have the right to represent the view of their constituents and vote on legislation at the House of Commons.

12.4 Chapter 3 – Statutory Interpretation

Question 1

Answer

Option A is correct. This is a clear example of the use of the courts using Parliament's definitions as correctly written and interpreting them literally.

Question 2

Answer

Option B is correct. By referring to the Act that is likely to form an important part of the case at hand, they have referred to an internal aid.

Question 3

Answer

Option C is correct. This is because the mischief that the Act is seeking to correct appears to be clear – the concept of cleaner air by lowering toxic NO2 emissions. The fact that the rickshaw is not mentioned is irrelevant – the government have been clear in their rationale and that appears to also be in the preamble.

12.5 Chapter 4 – Judicial Structures Within the Courts

Question 1

Answer

Option A is correct. Employment Tribunals do allow for non-legal personnel, with the required training to assist judges by being subject experts. The Crown Court will only utilise legally qualified circuit judges or recorders.

Question 2

Answer

Option B is correct. A jury will listen to the evidence and determine guilt. The Old Bailey is the Central Criminal Court, housing the Crown Court. The offence is also stated as an indictable one. The circuit judge will not decide guilt – they are there to advise the jury and sentence.

Question 3

Answer

Option A is correct. Judges must make a decision based upon evidence and submissions that have been made by both parties.

12.6 Chapter 5 – Sources of Law – The Courts and Precedent

Question 1

Answer

Option B is correct. Parliament is supreme, and judges have a duty to apply the law as it appears in the statute book – notwithstanding the manner in which the Act has been passed. Judges must ensure that they are not taking on the role of law makers, but questioning the validity of an Act of Parliament, as stated in Dicey's theory of Parliamentary Supremacy and the enrolled Bill rule.

Question 2

Answer

Option C is correct. There are three exceptions to the rule standard rule that the Court of Appeal is bound by its own previous decisions. One is precisely that whereby there are two conflicting precedents. The judges will choose the correct one, and that one will be precedent moving forward.

Question 3

Answer

Option B is correct. High Court Judges, whilst encouraged to follow precedent set at the same level, are not required to follow this mandatorily. The question of the Act of Parliament is not clear – Royal Assent does not signify legislation coming into force – this is usually made clear in the Act, and could come into force at a later date.

Thus, it is important to note that the judge must apply the law *as is* on the day.

12.7 Chapter 6 – Civil Courts

Question 1

Answer

Option D is correct.

According to Practice Direction (PD) 7A of the Civil Procedure Rules (CPR), a personal injury claim with a value of more than £50,000 can be commenced in either the county court or the High Court. Paragraph 2.4 of the PD states that a case should only be started in the High Court if the following factors indicate that this is appropriate:

1) the financial value of the claim and the amount in dispute, and/or
2) the complexity of the facts, legal issues, remedies or procedures involved, and/or
3) the importance of the outcome of the claim to the public in general.

In the question it is clear that the claim is a simple and straightforward matter and a correct interpretation of CPR PD 7A would result in the claim commencing in the county court.

Question 2

Answer

Option E is correct.

The matter should be commenced in the Patents Court, which is part of the Chancery Division of the High Court. This court has the relevant jurisdiction for breach of patent claims where the claim value is in excess of £500,000. The correct remedies in the case would be in the form of damages and the destruction of the counterfeits.

Question 3

Answer

Option A is correct.

Both the Court of Appeal and the Supreme Court have jurisdiction to grant a right of appeal in the case with the case then progressing to the Supreme Court for determination.

12.8 Chapter 7 – Criminal Courts

Question 1

Answer

Option C is correct. Appeals that are made by way of case stated are those where Magistrates or a District Judge has erred in the application of the law. In the event the appeal is refused by the divisional court in the King's Bench Division, an application can be made to the Supreme Court.

Question 2

Answer

Option E is correct. The defence can appeal from the Crown Court to the Court of Appeal where the sentence is manifestly excessive.

Question 3

Answer

Option C is correct. The woman is being tried for an offence triable only on indictment and will be sent for trial at the Crown Court at the first available opportunity. The trial will be in front of a judge and jury.

12.9 Chapter 8 – Regulating Legal Services

Question 1

Answer

Option B is correct. Within the regulatory framework set down by the Legal Services Act 2007 the firm must be authorised by an approved regulator, overseen by the Legal Services Board.

Question 2

Answer

Option D is correct. An authorised provider must abide by the regulations set forth by their own regulator (in this case, the SRA) for all legal services rendered, not simply those that fit into the category of reserved legal activities.

12.10 Chapter 9 – Overriding Legal Obligations

Question 1

Answer

Option A is correct. His line manager's behaviour amounts to harassment under the Act. The line manager's behaviour occurred in the course of their employment and so the firm will also be vicariously liable.

Question 2

Answer

Option C is correct. As a general rule verification should be obtained at first contact.

Verification must be obtained from a reliable source which is independent from the client. The letter would not fall within this description. Good practice dictates that verification should be based on at least one government document. The cash payment proposal should be concerning. The solicitor should refuse to act in these circumstances.

Question 3

Answer

Option E is the best answer. Despite the fact that the suspected illegal behaviour occurred outside of the UK (tax fraud is a crime in Spain) no conviction is necessary – only suspicion – an authorised disclosure was necessary to avoid breaking s. 328. But merely making an authorised disclosure cannot be utilised as a defence. Even after disclosing the information, the solicitor will still be in violation because they went ahead and executed the purchase without permission. The designated officer is responsible for filing a suspicious activity report, and the solicitor's liability under section 328 is unaffected by the officer's failure to file the report.

12.11 Chapter 10 – Financial Services

Question 1

Answer

Option B is the correct answer. In the scenario provided, a number of key tests need to be considered, and these are as follows:

- The client seeks advice and assistance from the solicitor who is 'in business.'
- Shares in a private company are a specified investment.
- In acting as the client requests the solicitor will be carrying out the specified investment activities of advising and arranging.

To avoid a breach of section 19 of FSMA 2000, the solicitor will need to rely on an exclusion or exemption.

With a shareholding of 75% and the arrangements involving sale to a fellow director, the takeover exclusion applies.

Question 2

Answer

Option C is correct. You will not be in violation of FSMA 2000 by providing the advice as property/land is not a specified investment. But, it is clear that you are not competent or qualified to give the advice in the first instance. As a result, you will be in violation of Paragraph 3.2 of the SRA's Code of Conduct and could face disciplinary action. It would not be ethical or in the client's best interests to offer advice when you are not capable of doing so.

Question 3

Answer

Option C is the best fit. While you have received a pecuniary award and have 'arranged' the investment, as it currently stands, crypto assets are not deemed to be specified investments under the Financial Services and Markets Act 2000.

12.12 Chapter 11 – Funding Legal Services

Question 1

Answer

Option B is correct. This is a 'no win, no fee' CFA, so if the client loses, they will not have to pay anything in fees, but will still be liable for disbursements (and the opponent's costs). In a CFA the success fee is calculated as a percentage of the usual charging rate, not a percentage of the damages received. If the client wins, they will have to pay the success fee as it cannot be recovered from the opponent.

Question 2

Answer

Option B is correct. It is for the client to decide how their costs are funded, but there is no obligation on you and the firm to act for a client on a particular basis. Therefore, a firm may refuse to act under a DBA as a matter of policy. A junior solicitor should always adhere to the firm's policy even in cases like this where the risk might be low. If it is in the client's best interests to have a DBA and your company do not utilise these methods of funding, then you should send them elsewhere, or at least get clarification on the matter.

Question 3

Answer

Option B is correct. they must still satisfy the merits test and the capital element of the means test. On these facts the client satisfies both the merits test and the means tests, as the client is in receipt of welfare benefits and has no savings.

Index

access to justice 7, 9, 76, 87, 121, 169, 171
acquisition, use or possession 145, 147, 151, 157
Acts of Parliament 21, 22, 25, 26, 30, 33, 72, 78
Acts of Union 1706–07 24
adequate and appropriate insurance 124
affirmative resolution procedure 32
after-the-event insurance 169, 170
age discrimination 128
alternative business structures 138
arranging 145, 146, 156, 157
authorisation 122, 123; admission 124; of individuals 122; licensed bodies 122; practising certificates 124
authorised firms, Indemnity Insurance Rules 124, 125
authorised third persons 156

before-the-event insurance 169
Bill of Rights 1689 15, 21, 22
Bingham, Lord 7, 22, 47

chartered accountants 122
civil legal aid 171; legal representation 171; means test 172; merits test 172
comparator, direct discrimination 132, 133, 135
concealing offence 145, 146
conditional fee agreement (CFA) 167, 169
confidentiality 147
constitutional conventions 16; Parliamentary sovereignty, and 13, 21, 23, 44, 51, 72; purpose of 16
constitutional conventions 16
Constitutional Reform Act 2005 7, 10, 15, 59, 61, 66, 67, 79, 96
constitutional statutes, repeal of 21, 22; judicial review, and 24; law reform 24; legal authority for state actions 24; legislative sources of 24; royal prerogative 24; rule of law, and 24; separation of powers, and 24; sources of 24; sovereignty of Parliamentary, and 24; types of 24
Constitutions 15
consumer credit activities 152
Coronavirus Act 2020 25
criminal legal aid 172; interests of justice test 173
cross-examination of witnesses 109, 173

damages, and claims 62, 73, 88, 90, 128, 133, 165, 168, 172
damages-based agreement (DBA) 168, 169, 170
declaration 11, 128
defence 105, 109, 110, 111, 122, 128, 146, 147
delegated legislation 31
democratic society, rights necessary in 130
devolution 22, 33
devolved power 33; Northern Ireland 24, 25, 33; Scotland 33; Wales 33

Dicey, AV 7, 12, 21, 24
direct discrimination 132; comparator 132; less favourable treatment 132; protected characteristics 132
disability discrimination 134, 135
disclosure 106, 107, 146, 160
discrimination, protection from 128
discrimination *see* Equality Act 2010
diversity 121
duty to make adjustments 137, 138; auxiliary aid provision 138; provision, criterion or practice 137

elections 11, 26, 27
embryos/foetuses 47
Employment Tribunal 60, 61, 77, 128
enhanced due diligence 143
Enrolled Bill rule 21, 22
equality 7, 12, 121
Equality Act 2010 42, 127, 128, 131, 134, 135, 136, 137, 138, 139; age 128; Barristers 121; direct discrimination 132; disability 128; disability discrimination 134; discrimination under 127; duty to make adjustments 137, 138; gender reassignment 129; harassment 135; indirect discrimination 133; marriage/ civil partnerships 129; overlap with professional conduct 136, 137, 138, 139; physical features 128, 138; positive action 137; pregnancy and maternity 131; prohibited conduct 132; protected characteristics 128; provision, criterion or practice 133, 134; provision of auxiliary aid 138; race 129; religion and belief 130; sex 131; sexual orientation 131; solicitors as employers 135; solicitors as service providers 136; victimisation 136
Equality and Human Rights Commission (EHRC) 131
equality before the law 7
equal pay 127, 132
European Convention on Human Rights (ECHR) 10; accordance with law, qualification of rights in 10
exemption for professional firms, financial services 156; 'incidental' 159; no other regulated activities 143; not prohibited 125, 152; 'pecuniary or other advantage' 159; permitted regulated activities only 154
express repeal, doctrine of 23
extradition 90, 106

fair trial 6, 65
Financial Action Task Force 140
Financial Conduct Authority 125, 152, 153, 159
financial promotion prohibition 153, 154; consumer credit activities 154; exemption for professional firms 154; general prohibition 154; 'incidental' 154; no other regulated activities 154; not prohibited 154; 'pecuniary or other advantage' 154; permitted regulated activities only 154
firm-based authorisation, SRA 123
fixed fees 165, 166, 167
funding civil litigation 165; legal expense insurance 169; solicitor and client costs and costs between parties 165; third party funding 170; variable fees 165
funding options: after-the-event insurance 169; before-the-event insurance 169; conditional fee agreement 167; damages-based agreement 168; fixed fees 166

gender reassignment, and discrimination 128, 129, 135
general elections 26

habeas corpus 8, 90
harassment 127, 132, 135, 136, 137
horizontal effect 12

House of Commons 25, 26, 27, 28, 32, 72
House of Lords 26, 27, 28, 61, 75, 76, 79, 96
Human Rights Act 1998 15, 22, 24
Hunting Act 2004 27, 28

identity 142, 143
immunity 10
implied repeal, doctrine of 21, 22, 23
indirect discrimination 132, 133, 134, 135
injunctions 62, 90, 128
Insolvency Practitioners Association 125
intimidation 111

Judicial Appointments Commission 10, 62, 63, 64, 66
judicial review, generally 14, 15, 32, 90, 93
judiciary: appointments 66, 67; executive, relationship with 59; immunity of 10; independence and impartiality 67; legislature, relationship with 59

Law Society 120, 159
legal aid 165, 166, 171; civil legal aid 171; criminal legal aid 172; legal certainty 173; means test 172; merits test 172; scope of legal aid 171; statutory charge 172
legal services 120; authorisation 122; definition of 120; regulation of 120; reserved legal activities 122
Legal Services Board 121
Legislature 21; executive, relationship with 22; judiciary, relationship with 22; separation of powers 22
legitimacy 14
less favourable treatment 132, 133, 135
licensed bodies 122
licensed conveyancers 121
life peers 27
litigation, conduct of 68, 122, 167, 168
Lord Chancellor 59
Lord Chief Justice 59, 60, 63, 77

Magna Carta 1215 5, 8, 9, 15
marriage/civil partnerships, and discrimination 128, 129
ministerial responsibility 16
monarchy 9, 10, 33; Crown immunity 10; role and powers of 10; royal prerogative 10
money laundering 127, 139; client account 141; client due diligence 142; enhanced due diligence 143; ongoing monitoring 142; requirement for 142; simplified due diligence 143; standard due diligence 143
Money Laundering Compliance Officer (MLCO) 141
Money Laundering Reporting Officer (MLRO) 141, 144
Money Laundering, Terrorist Financing and Transfer of Funds (Information on the Payer) Regulations 2017 127, 139; application of 139, 140; policies, controls and procedures 140; purpose of 139; real estate 140; record keeping 144; relevance and significance for solicitors 144; risk assessment 142; training 142

National Crime Agency 141, 144, 146
natural justice 113
negative procedure 32
Northern Ireland 24, 25, 33, 54, 66, 67, 81, 97
notarial activities 122
notaries 63, 65, 122

oaths, administration of 122
offences, overview of 145
Office of the Immigration Services Commissioner 95, 125
ouster clauses 51

parliament 21, 26; collective cabinet responsibility 8, 16; composition 26; delegated legislation 31; elections 11, 26;

executive–legislature, relationships between government ministers, restrictions on 14; House of Commons 26; House of Lords 26
Parliament Acts 1911 and 1949 25, 27, 30
partnerships 143
patent attorneys 121
penalties 68, 107
politically exposed person (PEP) 144
practising certificates 124, 125
pregnancy and maternity, and discrimination 128, 131, 134
private bills 25, 27, 33
private funding 165, 166
private members' bills 25
probate activities 122, 156
Proceeds of Crime Act 2002 145
professional indemnity insurance 124, 125
'professional/necessary' exclusion 157, 158, 160
prohibited conduct, under Equality Act 2010 132; comparator 132; direct discrimination 132; disability discrimination 132; harassment 135; indirect discrimination 133; less favourable treatment 133; protected characteristics 128; victimisation 136
proportionality 54, 172
protected characteristics 128; age 128; direct discrimination 132; disability 128; gender reassignment 129; marriage/ civil partnerships 129; pregnancy and maternity 131; race 129; religion and belief 130; sex 131; sexual orientation 131
Prudential Regulation Authority 152, 153
public bills 25

race, and discrimination 128, 129
recognised body 122; authorisation 122
record keeping, and money laundering 141, 142
regulated activity, and financial services 153, 154; advising 156, 157, 158; arranging 156, 157; authorised third persons 156; business test 154; dealing as agent 153, 155, 156, 157; exclusions 156; execution-only client 156; introducing 156; management 155, 156, 157, 158; 'professional/ necessary' exclusion 156; safeguarding 155, 156, 157, 158; specified investment activities 155; takeover exclusion 157; trustees or personal representatives 156
religion and belief, and discrimination 128, 130
remedies 62, 76
repeal of statutes 21, 22, 23, 26
retained EU law 12, 13
right of audience, exercise of 63, 93, 94, 122, 123
right to fair trial 6
right to free elections 11
right to liberty 80, 173
risk-based regulation, SRA as 120, 121
Royal Assent 9, 16, 22, 25, 26, 27, 28, 29, 30, 33, 34
royal prerogative 15, 16
rule of law, and 6, 7, 8, 10, 76, 121

same-sex partners, rights of 129
Scottish Parliament 22, 25
sex, and discrimination 131
sexual orientation, and discrimination 131
simplified due diligence 143
sole practitioner 138
Solicitors Regulation Authority (SRA) 120, 153; adequate and appropriate insurance 124; admission 122; authorisation of individuals 122; client information 122; effect of 122; firm-based authorisation 122; practising certificates 122;

process 121; professional indemnity insurance 124
sovereignty of Parliament, and 13, 21, 22, 25, 41, 44, 51, 72
specified investment activities 155; advising 156; arranging 156; dealing as agent 155; management 156; safeguarding 156
SRA Financial Services (Conduct of Business) Rules 159
SRA Indemnity Insurance Rules 94, 124, 125; risk-based regulation 123; role in money laundering 120
standard due diligence 143
statutory instruments 26, 31, 32, 106, 152
Supreme Court, references to 97; Appeals 97, 112
suspicious activity report 141, 144, 146
takeover exclusion 157
tipping off, money laundering 146; defences 146; offences 146; penalties 146
training, and money laundering 147
treaties 12, 16, 53
trustees or personal representatives 157

ultra vires 14, 32
unregulated providers 125
unwanted conduct 135

victimisation 132, 136, 137

Wales 33; legislative powers 33; Devolution 33; National Assembly 33

For Product Safety Concerns and Information please contact our
EU representative GPSR@taylorandfrancis.com Taylor & Francis
Verlag GmbH, Kaufingerstraße 24, 80331 München, Germany